Critical Guides to Spanish Texts

55 Laforet: Nada

Critical Guides to Spanish Texts

EDITED BY J.E. VAREY, A.D. DEYERMOND AND C. DAVIES

LAFORET

Nada

Barry Jordan

Lecturer in Spanish
University of Nottingham

Grant & Cutler Ltd
in association with Tamesis Books Ltd

© Grant & Cutler Ltd 1993

ISBN 0 7293 03330 6

I.S.B.N. 84-599-3307-5

DEPÓSITO LEGAL: V. 213-1993

Printed in Spain by
Artes Gráficas Soler, S.A., Valencia
for
GRANT & CUTLER LTD
55-57 GREAT MARLBOROUGH STREET, LONDON WIV 2AY

Contents

Preface

My primary aim in writing this Critical Guide has been to provide a detailed textual study of Carmen Laforet's best-known novel. For this reason, I have paid relatively little attention to Laforet's other works and to matters of context, background, sources and influences. This is not because I believe such work is not valuable; indeed, most of my own scholarly work has had to do with the interface between text and context. Nor do I hold the view that the text in itself contains everything the reader needs to know in order to appreciate it. My concentration on the text responds to the fact that, in the preparation of this study, several new and challenging topics have come to light, topics which I did not anticipate and which have demanded further exploration, e.g. the role of the gaze, confessional writing, *Nada* as an example of a literature of desire and so on. Thus, while I have endeavoured to comment on the obvious topics of critical interest, e.g. narrative perspective, character, style, themes etc., I have also tried to extend the boundaries of critical interpretation a little and open up some new ground. Where this work has involved the use of terms from other kinds of discourse, e.g. psychoanalysis, I have tried as far as possible to gloss those unfamiliar items and refer the reader to helpful bibliography.

Criticism of Laforet's fictional work as a whole is not particularly extensive though, as one might expect, *Nada* has attracted by far the largest part of it. I have tried to take into account the main critical writings on the novel, as well as review material culled from Spanish newspapers and magazines of the 1940s and 50s. However, this study should not be regarded as a guide to existing criticism. Indeed, part of the reason for producing it has been my own dissatisfaction and disagreement with much of the available criticism and its tendency to regard *Nada*, often quite unproblematically, as a success story. That is, as a novel of female development, in which the protagonist is said to reach maturity and achieve a secure, stable identity. I take issue with this approach, partly because of the fact that the terms it employs are rarely fully explained, e.g. female development, maturity, adulthood, identity. Also, to accept the novel's 'happy ending' at face value is to engage in a superficial reading which simplifies a much more ambiguous, contradictory and interesting narrative. I wish to stress, therefore, the contradictory and challenging nature of Laforet's novel. This may be unhelpful to those readers, especially those preparing the novel for examinations, who are looking for a straightforward, simplified *explication de texte*. But contradiction and uncertainty are fundamental to Laforet's novel and only by grappling with the text's absences, paradoxes and annoying ellipses are we likely to do it justice and enjoy its many narrative pleasures.

All references to the text of *Nada* are taken from the second Destinolibro paperback edition (Barcelona, July 1980) on the assumption that this is the edition most readers are likely to buy and use. In any case, as far as I can tell, this edition is a reprint of the first edition of May 1945. There does exist an American college edition of the novel, but because of its abridged nature it is not recommended for use (*1*).

The figures in parentheses in italic type refer to the numbered items in the Bibliographical Note; where appropriate, the italicized figures are followed by page numbers.

I should like to express my gratitude to the editors of this series, Professors J.E. Varey and A.D. Deyermond, for their painstaking correction of my MS. and their many useful comments and suggestions. I would also like to thank Dr Anthony Clarke, Department of Hispanic Studies, University of Birmingham, for his help and encouragement in the final stages of this study.

1. Introduction

Carmen Laforet began her writing career in the early 1940s but, for reasons which remain obscure, her production of fictional work came to a rather abrupt and unexpected halt in the early 1960s. Her creative output over a twenty-year period included four novels and a sizeable amount of short fiction. Since then, apart from a travelogue (*Paralelo 35*, 1967) and a collection of short novels (*La niña y otros relatos*, published in 1970, but written in the 1940s and 50s), her writing activity has been limited almost exclusively to occasional journalism. Despite this prolonged creative silence, unbroken to this day, Laforet has not been forgotten. Indeed, she is still regarded by critical opinion as a noteworthy figure in the development of contemporary Spanish literature and is invariably credited, alongside Cela and others, with having helped initiate the recovery of realism in the postwar novel. [1] Nonetheless, it is quite clear that her lasting appeal as a writer derives almost exclusively from the extraordinary success of one novel, which has eclipsed the rest of her output and become almost synonymous with the writer herself. I refer, of course, to *Nada* (1945), her dark, brooding, enigmatically-entitled first novel, which won the first Nadal Literary Prize (1944) and made her famous.

It is now a critical commonplace to state that had it not been for the Nadal Prize, Laforet's literary career might well have taken a different direction or failed to get started at all. There is no doubt some truth in this. Also, of considerable importance in launching her career was the propitious historical and cultural context in which the novel first appeared. In the hungry, repressive, puritanical Spain of

---

[1] See for example, Santos Sanz Villanueva, *Historia de la novela social española 1942-1975*, I (Madrid: Alhambra, 1980), p.8.

the mid-1940s, *Nada* managed to articulate some of the needs of a reading public anxious to escape post-war privations and recapture the certainties of a more settled, prosperous pre-war society. The prize, the attendant publicity and a specific context of popular reading tastes all combined to hoist a totally unknown 23-year old female law student to national prominence and literary acclaim. Yet despite Nadal-sponsored stardom, perhaps even because of the public expectations and pressures it created for the author, Laforet failed to consolidate and build on her early success. After *Nada*, her output was somewhat erratic, marked by lengthy gaps between publications; but, at the same time, her creative work was held together by the exploration of certain dominant, recurrent concerns.

  Nada, as is well known, is a first-person narrative in which the orphan Andrea, who is both protagonist and narrator, imaginatively reconstructs her experience of spending a year with her mother's family in Calle Aribau. During her stay, she attends University and develops a series of friendships with her fellow students. Set in Barcelona just after the Civil War, the novel charts Andrea's attempts to recapture the happiness and optimism of her childhood memories and at the same time to achieve independence, emotional fulfilment and a secure identity. The main setting for this search is, of course, the family, symbolized by two contrasting bourgeois households, one in terminal decline, the other increasingly prosperous. Calle Aribau, on the one hand, represents a family in crisis, apparently owing to the effects of the Civil War; but the problems go much deeper. Vía Layetana, on the other hand, home of Andrea's close friend Ena, is the exact opposite of Aribau: it represents the model family of the new Francoist order, drawn from Spain's entrepreneurial elite. Andrea is the reader's guide to both households and through her are revealed some of the secrets underlying the decline and fall of Aribau as well as the unexpected connections it has maintained in the past with Ena's family, into which Andrea is finally incorporated, on moving to Madrid at the end of the novel. *Nada* expresses a powerful yearning for the imagined stability and self-confidence of the turn-of-the-century bourgeoisie, its well-appointed apartments, velvet curtains, gentility, sophistication and taste in classical art. But it is principally concerned with the fears and difficulties of growing up and the gaining of an identity. In the end, Andrea opts not for mature womanhood and heterosexual relations, but for female friendship and the innocence of pre-adolescent sexuality.

Laforet's second novel, *La isla y los demonios* (1952), is also concerned with a young girl's search for identity and emotional fulfilment. Set in the Canary Islands, it stands as a kind of preparation to *Nada.* though it was written afterwards. It shows many obvious similarities with the earlier novel in structure, character relationships and themes. Where it differs is in the narrative perspective on events, now seen through a third-person, omniscient narrator rather than a first-person voice. In the third novel, *La mujer nueva* (1955), the figure of the young female protagonist, found in the previous two novels, is replaced by a much older married woman, Paulina (a name evocative of that of St Paul); and, as before, through a third-person narrative voice, the novel shows how the protagonist achieves a certain degree of security and self-confidence by way of a sudden conversion to Catholicism. Laforet's fourth and final novel, *La insolación* (1963), which forms the first part of a projected but uncompleted trilogy (*Tres pasos fuera del tiempo*), returns to the island setting of the Canaries and to an adolescent main protagonist, but this time male not female. Exploiting the workings of fantasy and dreams, the novel charts the young Martín Soto's passage towards self-affirmation and male maturity, through family and youthful relationships, focusing in particular on the formation of male sexual identity.

In general, in the novels and to a considerable extent in the short stories, Laforet repeatedly explores the social and, more importantly, the psycho-sexual development of mainly young, mainly female characters. Their search for selfhood, security and a stable identity is dramatized predominantly through a series of encounters with exceptional or unusual characters, who act as role models. In the process of interaction, however, the protagonists' search for a stable self seems to be put consistently in doubt. The self always appears to be open to disruption, always ambivalently poised between one model of behaviour and another, always internally riven between reason and unreason, will and desire, decorum and the sexual drives. Such concerns, as we shall see later, find their earliest and perhaps most intriguing treatment in *Nada*.

2. Story and Structure

The formal structure of *Nada* is quite clear: 25 chapters, grouped into 3 separate parts containing 9, 9 and 7 chapters respectively. In purely quantitative terms, the novel displays a fairly even and consciously organized arrangement of material. This impression of order is further enhanced by the reasonably balanced chronological coverage of Andrea's year in Barcelona in each of the three parts: Part I covers October to February, Part II March to June and Part III July to September. (It is worth pointing out, however, that chronological and temporal markers in the novel are left rather vague and shadowy, suggesting that we are not dealing with a conventional memoir or diary.) *Nada* has also an identifiable beginning and end, encompassed by the main protagonist's arrival and departure; it thus gives the impression of a complete process. These signs of proportionality and coherence in the distribution of material may, however, be somewhat misleading. For example, there is something rather arbitrary about the author's choice of a tripartite division for the novel. There certainly seem to be valid reasons for the break between Parts I and II. At the end of Part I, Angustias departs for the convent, thus releasing Andrea from her control and surveillance and allowing her to enjoy her freedom and indulge her whims; a significant change has taken place in the action and we enter a new situation, signalled by the shift into Part II. However, the break between Parts II and III is puzzling and seems not to respond to any significant change in the narrative logic or chain of causality in the events of the novel. At the end of Part II, Andrea bumps into Ena's mother, Margarita, just as she is leaving the flat in Aribau; at the beginning of Part III, the encounter is smoothly and straightforwardly continued in the café with Margarita's confession to Andrea. Unlike the situation at the end of Part I, there is no culmination of one narrative sequence nor the beginning of another between Parts II and III; nor is there any significant change of direction. There seems to be no good structural reason to warrant a break. It may be doubted, therefore, if the novel's tripartite division is as crucial as most critics claim.

Nada follows a straightforward linear, chronological development, yet it is by no means a simple matter to provide a detailed outline of the story. Paradoxically, despite its highly visible formal structure, *Nada* remains a largely plotless, eventless novel, with no dominant narrative thread, except perhaps that of the main protagonist's personal experience during her year-long stay at her grandmother's. But, even here, Andrea's function as protagonist and structuring element is ambiguous, since she invariably drops out of sight and adopts the role of observer, eavesdropper and voyeur. In this sense, she does very little; she is not the sort of active protagonist who influences the course of events. Indeed, they influence and structure her. In this regard, many of the incidents in the novel (Andrea's visits to the University, Ena's house, the coast, the *barrio gótico*, etc.), could probably be transposed or eliminated completely without radically altering the story line, such as it is. And though there appears to be some plot development, in the sense that Andrea seemingly fulfils her dream of reincorporation into a stable bourgeois family, the impression is given of a novel comprising an almost random set of events. Indeed, material in the form of visits, encounters, memories, confessions, and other embedded stories tends to be presented in a dispersed, fragmentary fashion. Chapters usually consist of several different scenes and their arrangement and sequencing seem to correspond to the playful vagaries of the narrator's moods and memories. In fact, the dominant note struck by the narrator of the story is that of haziness and uncertainty. This partly responds to Laforet's attempt to present events through the innocent eyes of the young Andrea; it also functions as a strategy to create an atmosphere of mystery and intrigue. But at the same time, it is as if the narrator, the older, wiser Andrea who recounts her experience of the past, is unwilling to take responsibility for the version of events she offers the reader. Textual dispersion and narratorial relativism (i.e. the lack of an authoritative, reliable, narrative voice) are complemented by *Nada's* elliptical quality, that is, its tendency to withhold information, leave gaps and ends untied and enigmas unresolved as the story unfolds (why did Román commit suicide? what happened to him in prison? why is Andrea so passive at Aribau after being regarded as rebellious and uncontrollable by her cousin Isabel? why did Angustias cease to concern herself with Andrea's moral education? what caused the economic decline of Aribau? what happened to Andrea's parents?). There is thus a significant surplus of non-narrated story activity in *Nada* and a whole series of questions which receive no adequate response and which, of course, add mystery and piquancy to the act of reading.

Despite the novel's loose, baggy, elliptical arrangement, critics have insisted on the importance of its tripartite structural division. I leave to a later chapter an extended discussion of the dominant critical view on this matter, but it may be worth briefly introducing it now. A number of critics have made the reasonable but quite mechanical assumption that the three parts of the novel correspond to three broad stages or phases in the gradual development of the main protagonist towards maturity and adulthood. Michael Thomas, for example, regards the novel's three-fold structure in terms of Andrea's transition from enclosure (Part I), through liberation (Part II) towards clarification (Part III) (*27*, pp.57-58); Robert Spires takes a similar view, but interprets the three parts according to the schema of darkness (I), light (II) and greyness (III), arguing that Part III reveals the interplay of two opposed worlds (*25*, pp.72-73); Juan Villegas notes a similarity between the novel's tripartite structure and the basic structure of the traditional folk tale, interpreting *Nada* according to Vladimir Propp's folk-tale morphology (*30*, pp.178-79); Johnson, by contrast, regards the novel's structure as much looser and full of gaps and absences (*6*, p.50); Ruth El Saffar rejects the idea of Andrea's progressive maturation and emphasizes, not cumulative development, but the novel's circularity and layering, which is reinforced by its many parallels, oppositions, contrasts and above all, repetitions (*10*, p.121). My interpretation of the novel inclines more towards El Saffar than to Thomas. A simple indicator of this is seen in the way any sense of progressive development in the protagonist towards freedom and independence is invariably offset, if not subverted, by a counter event, force or movement. For example, there is the cruel reversal of expectations at Pons's ball; also, Andrea occupies Angustias's room and believes that at last she has found a space of her own, only to find that it is regularly invaded by Román. We thus find in the novel a certain see-saw effect, a dynamic interplay in which progress towards freedom is cancelled out by regression. Indeed, Andrea's sense of achieving a unified, stable self, which is free of the repressions of the older generation, seems to be indefinitely suspended by one frustration after another. In short, the idea of Andrea's development towards adulthood and maturity as a function of the novel's three-fold structure may be more apparent than real. It may well mask, as I shall argue later, a situation in which Andrea, far from moving forward in emotional and psycho-sexual terms, is actually marking time, running on the spot and in the end, going nowhere.

Rather than pursue the dominant model of linear progress, a more fruitful approach to the question of the novel's organization lies, in my view, in a sensitive reading of the many significant coincidences, parallels, contrasts, reversals, and repetitions, which litter the text and which can be derived from the following plot summary.

Part I of *Nada* opens with Andrea's delayed midnight arrival by train at Barcelona. (The delay is crucial in allowing her to experience her arrival as a liberation, since she is not met by her aunt Angustias and escorted to Aribau; the time of arrival is also crucial in enhancing the atmosphere of Gothic tale and mystery story and in letting Andrea challenge a major taboo: the prohibition against a young woman being alone at night in a major city. Furthermore, let us not forget that at the end of Part I, Angustias departs for the convent by train and in Part III Ena leaves for Madrid by train; these are obvious parallels and echo Angustias's injunction concerning the twin destinies for women: marriage or the convent). Of course, as in all good romances, Andrea's initial experience of freedom is short-lived and her euphoria at returning to the city of her childhood dreams (she was last in Barcelona when she was seven, i.e. eleven years previously) is immediately shattered by her reception at the flat in Aribau, inhabited by her relatives. There, she is confronted, not with the prosperous bourgeois residence of her childhood memories and adolescent fantasies, but with its ghastly post-war opposite: a house of darkness, filth, decay, stifling atmosphere, and bizarre, ghostly inhabitants, survivors from an older generation, animal as well as human. Andrea thus enters, not a place of stability and freedom, but one of conflict, confinement and unreason, as exemplified in the behaviour of her adopted family: eccentric, cruel, violent and hysterical. *Nada* thus begins on a note of severe disruption and instability, especially in relation to the order of the family, which has been inexplicably undermined and replaced by anarchy. The purpose of the story, in broad terms, will be to recount the recuperation of stability and the re-establishment of a second equilibrium, similar to the first (as symbolized by Andrea's childhood memories), but also differently located in geographical, class, family, and emotional terms. However, as previously argued, *Nada* contains few significant events which mark and advance the story of that recovery. In fact, the novel's forward chronological movement is accompanied by and arguably over-determined by a backwards pull, a nostalgic re-examination of the past. In this, Andrea acts as the reader's non-too-reliable guide to the secrets underlying the collapse of Aribau and its uncanny past links with Ena's family. In a sense, the way forward for Andrea is a journey backwards, her recovery of stability and an identity being a function of searching out and purging the effects of the past. In short, her path to maturity is predicated on a return of the repressed, on a necessary confrontation with the many skeletons and secrets guarded by Aribau.

Several narrative strands emerge in Part I: i) The attempt by Andrea's aunt Angustias to impose on her niece the repressive habits and values of traditional bourgeois respectability, family honour and class exclusivity — in fact to inflict on Andrea the very education she herself received from her mother. Angustias also tries to impose on Andrea the sort of restrictions and controls she herself should be exercising in relation to her affair with Jerónimo Sanz; that is, she makes Andrea the scapegoat for her own guilt feelings. ii) Andrea's passive resistance to her aunt's will and her exposure to other characters of the house by direct contact and conversations as well as through reported stories. In particular, like other female figures in the novel (Margarita, Gloria, Antonia, Ena), Andrea experiences an early infatuation with the handsome, talented, but cruel and perverse Román, who takes great pleasure in causing conflict between his brother Juan and sister-in-law Gloria, as if avenging himself on them. iii) The traces of Aribau's historical decline which are extremely vague but which suggest the loss of the male head of household at the beginning of the Civil War and the family's fall into anarchy and decay after hostilities. iv) Andrea's initial contacts with the outside world, her University friendships, especially her relationship with Ena — fascinating, coquettish, egotistical and, like her male counterpart Román, calculating and sadistic. We also see Andrea's vain attempts to keep her two worlds apart, that is, to hide from her rich University friends the 'realidad miserable' (63) of Aribau. However, as has happened in the past, these worlds are destined to merge; the dramas and conflicts of the past will be re-staged, the old desires and misrecognitions repeated in the younger generation; and as the repressed is revisited and replayed, *Nada* warns the reader of the danger of romantic illusions, the deceptive nature of appearances and the threat posed to young women by male sexuality.

Looking at Part I in slightly greater detail, we see that Angustias's oppressive treatment of Andrea pushes the youngster to seek an outlet and a symbol of non-conformity in her uncle Román. Indeed, Andrea's initial infatuation with this satanic hero is but a further re-enactment of a role previously filled by other women in the novel, who have all fallen under Román's magic spell. Also, both characters deliberately collude in seeing in each other images of what they most desire: the talented, misunderstood artist and the intelligent, mature, vivacious young woman. They thus strive for confirmation of their hopes and fantasies, while being careful to hide their own insecurities and fears. As Andrea points out: 'Yo me daba cuenta de que él me creía una persona distinta; mucho más formada y tal vez más inteligente [...] No me gustaba desilusionarle, porque vagamente yo me sentía inferior; un poco insulsa con mis sueños y mi cara de sentimentalismo, que ante aquella gente procuraba ocultar' (39). As in other character relationships in the novel (for example, Margarita and Ena, the Abuela and her two sons), Román and Andrea mirror each other in trying to maintain appearances and in reinforcing each other's illusions. Soon after, Andrea learns from Gloria about the other Román, the cruel, sadistic figure who — after a war-time affair with Gloria and a period spent in prison — now seems bent on destroying her marriage to his brother Juan. Andrea thus occupies and replays a role previously filled by Gloria, details of whose story (her infatuation and love affair with Román, marriage to Juan, pregnancy, childbirth, fears of abandonment, status as orphan, arrival at Aribau and position as outsider and class inferior) are all recycled in various mixtures in the stories of the other female characters.

At University, Andrea is strongly attracted to Ena, a younger female version of Román, renowned for her malice, cruelty and physical beauty, who fulfils all of Andrea's fantasies of self-confidence and self-assertion. Ena is thus Andrea's alter ego, the active, uninhibited *femme fatale*, but she is also regarded as a confidante, someone receptive to the story of Aribau, which Andrea is so anxious to reveal. Yet, in a remarkably similar way to her dealings with Román, Andrea's sense of inferiority and shame about her background prevent her from speaking about Aribau and from correcting Ena's positively flattering view of Román. Here again, Andrea colludes in keeping up appearances, in reinforcing another character's illusory view of the world. However, she is acutely disconcerted by Ena's desire to meet Román. On the one hand, it means that Ena will be meeting an undesirable and a class inferior, who is bound to reveal the misery of Aribau; this is something about which Andrea is very uneasy. On the other, Ena will be entering a world and a story of which, so far, only Andrea has held the secret; in preference to hearing it from Andrea, however, Ena is confident enough to go and find out for herself. These tensions give rise to a temporary break between the two young women. Andrea becomes reimmersed in the turmoil of life in Aribau, including the chaos of Christmas Day, Angustias's unexpected absence and Andrea's transfer into her aunt's bedroom. Here, we see Andrea fulfilling one of her long-standing desires for comfort and privacy but its fulfilment is shortlived and is undermined by her uncle Román. Indeed, in his obsession with Angustias's private affairs, Román makes several forays into the spinster's bedroom, rifling through letters and a diary, thus, in turn, undermining Andrea's claim to independence, symbolized here by a room of her own. Román's actions thus subvert Andrea's desires for a 'vida nueva', which at every turn seem to be frustrated. None the less, she agrees to an invitation to visit Román's flat and there, at first hand, like other women before her, experiences her uncle's teasing, malicious, perverse, threatening side; when she has panicked, fled downstairs and taken refuge in bed, a timely, indeed a providential, phone call from Ena seems to save her from Román's malign influence. This suggests another role, drawn from fairy tale and folk literature, which Ena partially fulfils: that of mediator, saviour or good fairy; this is a part Ena will replay at the end of the novel when she invites Andrea to Madrid.

Part I closes with Angustias's early-morning departure by train for her new life of seclusion in a convent, a life to which she is totally unsuited, as everyone recognizes. Before leaving, however, she tells Andrea that there are only two paths for a woman in Spain, 'Dos únicos caminos honrosos'(101): marriage or entry into a convent. As Juan's highly eccentric behaviour on the station platform indicates, Angustias's decision is motivated not by a religious vocation but by guilt at betraying traditional family values through maintaining an impossible love affair with her employer, Jerónimo Sanz. In earlier times, Sanz was Angustias's suitor, but he was rejected by her father for being poor and of a lower social class. Later, he made a fortune abroad and got married, but he has continued to court Angustias in what appears to be an impossible affair. Angustias's saintliness and self-denial are thus the unfortunate outcome of frustrated love and desire: the latter underlie her masochistic insistence on defending a repressive and archaic patriarchal system, for which she is prepared to sacrifice her own

happiness. In structural terms, Part I is fairly coherent and well organized, offering a smaller-scale version of the novel as a whole. As
we have seen, Angustias's departure prefigures those of Ena and
Andrea in Part III and indicates one of the major choices for women
proposed in the novel. Also, Part I is characterized by a structural
movement which will be repeated in the other two Parts. I refer to
the see-saw dynamic mentioned above and to the fact that Andrea's
experience of Aribau as a place of enclosure and escape will be
continued in other locations. Finally, Part I sets up a number of
relationships, encounters and behaviours which will also be recycled
in the other two parts, suggesting that Aribau's present is inextricably
predetermined by the mistakes and illusions of the past.

     With Angustias's departure, in Part II Andrea begins to
develop her relationships beyond the confines of Aribau. She
resumes her relationship with Ena and, when that is temporarily
halted, she sees several young men. With Ena and her family,
Andrea fulfils one of her adolescent fantasies: she re-experiences the
model bourgeois household, the good family of which Aribau is the
decadent, degraded opposite. She rediscovers the grand apartment,
the musical soirées around the piano and the ideal family grouping
— this new family is numerically a carbon copy of Aribau: Ena and
her five brothers, all of them blond (in contrast to the dark figures of
Aribau), plus the handsome, liberal, father Luis and the mother,
Margarita, who is portrayed as being slightly out of place, 'un pájaro
extraño y raquítico' (121), as Andrea describes her. A simple and
obvious contrast is thus made between Vía Layetana, the apparently
happy, stable family to which Ena belongs, and the inhabitants of
Aribau: lugubrious, deranged, at war with each other, in short, in
crisis. Other oppositions between the two families are also brought
out, economic and class differences as well as emotional and
psychological ones: where Vía Layetana represents innocence,
moderation, beauty, decorum, and freedom, Aribau suggests repression, perversion, excess, ugliness, and dangerous desire. In fact, the
two households could be seen as simple projections of the fears and
fantasies that inhabit Andrea's psyche and the gap that exists
between her own desires and their ultimate satisfaction. From Gloria

we learn that Juan refuses to let her visit her sister in the *barrio gótico* because of her lower-class origins; however, such visits are vital since she is economically supporting both her husband and baby with her earnings from gambling at her sister's establishment. Juan, of course, is unaware that his wife's earnings are feeding his baby and subsidizing his vain attempts to paint decent pictures. Gloria's activities thus repeat the widespread motif in *Nada* of the supportive role of women, as is the case between the other married couple with children, Luis and Margarita. At the same time, Andrea learns of Ena's affair with Jaime, a not so young *señorito* whose lack of interest in business affairs and reputation as a man of leisure make him a highly unsuitable match for the daughter of the new entrepreneurial class. Once again, we see repeated a feature already evident in the fraught relationships between Sanz and Angustias, Juan and Gloria: the problems caused by trying to maintain social and class boundaries. For a while, Andrea finds ineffable happiness in the company of Ena and Jaime on their visits to the coast; yet, while she basks in the reflected glory cast by the two lovers, she suspects that Ena is simply exploiting her friendship and playing with her: 'Cree que no puedo prescindir de su amistad. ¡Qué equivocación! Juega conmigo como todo el mundo lo hace — pensé injustamente [...] a los que ella alienta para luego gozarse en verlos sufrir' (141). Interestingly, even in her most negative feelings towards Ena, Andrea is still prepared to doubt her own accusations, make allowances for her friend's behaviour, indulge her, and refuse to fully acknowledge her bad side. (This also happens in the case of Román at the end of the novel, when Andrea begins to think that he has been unfairly treated by Ena.) Nevertheless, hurt feelings result in another short break with Ena and in the interim, Andrea sets aside her imagined *ménage à trois* and begins to go out with young men.

Her first experience is provided by Gerardo who, at least for Andrea, resembles Angustias at her most oppressive and authoritarian. His fumbling attempt to kiss her triggers a powerful reaction of disgust and repulsion. With absolutely no experience of men, Andrea responds with fear and loathing to physical contact, surmising that Gerardo must be 'uno de los infinitos hombres que nacen sólo para sementales y junto a una mujer no entienden otra actitud que ésta' (145). Curiously, the only time Andrea feels happy with Gerardo is when he wipes the lipstick from the lips of the nude statue in the park. That is, he removes the traces of sensuality which, for Andrea, have defaced the statue and deprived it of its beauty. This relates to an obsessive concern in the novel to cleanse the female characters of the suspicion of sensuality and desire which constantly hangs over them. It also suggests that Andrea too, is disturbed by such suspicions and is unable to deal with displays of normal sexual behaviour. She thus interprets Gerardo's advances as predatory and wildly overreacts since she still operates on the basis of a hopelessly naive and inappropriate notion of romantic love. In a sense, she confirms Angustias's injunction: 'Toda prudencia en la conducta es poca, pues el diablo reviste tentadoras formas... Una joven en Barcelona debe ser como una fortaleza' (25-26). Meanwhile, Andrea is astonished to discover that Román and Ena (as occurred with her mother in the past) have made contact and have thus brought about the very thing she feared most: the merging of worlds. Once again, there follows a considerable cooling in the relationship between Andrea and Ena, during which time Andrea has her second experience with men, in the shape of Pons, the rich, feckless youngster who introduces her to his artistic young friends. Despite or perhaps because of their overt elitism, their arrogance and their ridiculous pose as 'rebeldes', Andrea finds herself deliriously happy in their company: 'Me encontraba muy bien allí; la inconsciencia absoluta, la descuidada felicidad de aquel ambiente me acariciaba el espíritu' (159). Furthermore, she thinks nothing of preparing the *merienda* for them, a further sign of the female's supporting role. Under the surface, however, Andrea is happy because these 'hijos de papá' make absolutely no demands on her as a sexual being; they reserve that function for the gypsy woman who poses for them. Andrea thus relates to the youngsters on the basis of friendship; she is not forced to occupy a role for which she is as yet inexperienced and unprepared.

From this point, the novel takes two main directions: First, Andrea is sent by the Abuela to mediate between Juan and Gloria in the much discussed descent into the *barrio gótico*; in fact, she does absolutely nothing. This mediating role will be repeated in Part III when she is asked by Margarita to protect Ena from Román. Second, Andrea also realizes a dream in her ascent to Pons's house and the summer ball, which marks the climax of Part II. The ball is an obvious recycling and ironic inversion of the Cinderella story, particularly in the way the famous glass slipper is transformed into a pair of old shoes, the latter being the very element which negates Andrea's chances of happiness — or so she thinks. Imagining that Pons's mother rejects her on account of her shoes (which come to symbolize her class inferiority), Andrea flees the ball (as she fled Román's flat) and in the end, feels ugly, ridiculous, out of place and abandoned. But there is evidence to suggest that she could have bought new shoes for the ball had she wanted to; she certainly had no reservations in buying a new blouse to attend one of Ena's musical evenings. A suspicion starts to emerge that Andrea may have brought disaster on herself and that, like Angustias, she has a certain masochistic streak. The reversal of expectations at the ball is yet another moment when potential fulfilment is undermined. Andrea now comes to realize that life for her is already predetermined: 'Unos seres nacen para vivir, otros para trabajar, otros para mirar la vida. Yo tenía un pequeño y ruin papel de espectadora. Imposible salirme de él. Imposible libertarme' (224). Andrea declares herself to be a victim of fate, yet, given her passivity and inertia, one wonders how far she actually colludes in her own entrapment; the point is that the position of the spectator is one of relative safety, a position which suits Andrea completely and which she does little to change. Part II ends with her meeting Ena's mother as she is leaving Aribau — yet another sign of the interconnectedness of the two worlds and a device to carry the reader into Part III.

The final part of the novel opens with Margarita's long confession to Andrea, which shows many parallels with Gloria's story (particularly with regard to the roles of wife and mother) and perhaps constitutes the model female story for the whole novel. Margarita, like the Abuela in Part II, now calls on Andrea to act as a mediator and protector; that is, she asks her to intervene between

Ena and Román in order to prevent a relationship from developing. Margarita thus wishes to spare her daughter the trauma she suffered in her own adolescent infatuation with Román twenty years previously. And in so doing, she tries to ensure that the sins of the mother are not visited on the daughter. At the prospect of being active, of actually doing rather than watching, Andrea is nervously excited: 'A mí, acostumbrada a dejar que la corriente de los acontecimientos me arrastrase por sí misma, me emocionaba un poco aquel actuar mío que parecía iba a forzarla...' (255). Yet, when she finally enters Román's garret, she finds Ena in no obvious danger: 'parecía muy tranquila, sentada y fumando' (257). On leaving, however, Andrea notices Román's right hand in his pocket and 'mi fantasía me hizo pensar en su negra pistola' (258); thinking Román might use his gun, Andrea jumps on him, smothers him and screams at Ena to run. Needless to say, Andrea makes a complete fool of herself and becomes the target of Ena's sarcasm: 'Andrea ¿por qué eres tan trágica, querida?' (259). Later, the two friends meet and make up. Ena proceeds to confess her real motives in seeing Román: to avenge her mother's past humiliations (by threatening to reveal Román's black-market activities) and also to enjoy the thrill of 'el juego apasionante en que se convertía aquello para mí [...] este duelo entre la frialdad y el dominio de los nervios de Román y mi propia malicia y seguridad' (267). Ena's childish cruelty is thus more than a match for Román's; the experienced dark lover is beaten at his own game, taken in by the wiles of a calculating, sadistic young woman, the *trompeur* is *trompé*, the older generation taught a lesson by the younger. However, we are not meant to conclude that Ena is merely sadistic. She proceeds to reveal that her aggressive, masculine behaviour is no more than a front to satisfy her mother's idea of her as a strong, wilful adolescent. Underneath, so Ena claims, she is really a nice girl, in love with Jaime; and it is Andrea who has helped her realize the nature of her true self: accommodating, supportive, anxious to settle down, etc., especially after the fascinating and cathartic experience of defeating Román.

The novel ends with Ena's departure by train for Madrid, followed by the unexpected suicide of Andrea's uncle Román, the

reasons for which are left unexplained. Was it because Gloria
denounced him to the police? Was it because Ena jilted him and also
threatened to reveal his underworld activities? Was it, as Andrea
suggests, a case of the walking dead returning to their graves?
Whatever the reason, the suicide precipitates the departure from
Aribau of Antonia the servant, who was secretly in love with Román
but who displaced her desire for her master onto his dog, Trueno,
which she carries off with her. At the same time, Juan is grief-
stricken, his pain at the loss of his brother 'impúdico, enloquecedor,
como el de una mujer por su amante, como el de una madre joven
por la muerte del primer hijo' (281). Juan's reaction seems to suggest
more than just brotherly love in his relationship with Román, and so
distraught and violent has he become that Gloria thinks seriously of
committing him to a lunatic asylum. Andrea, whose prospects are
rather bleak, seems resigned to spending another year in Barcelona
until she receives a letter from Ena inviting her to come to Madrid
and take a job in her father's business while finishing her degree.
And this she does. Collected one morning in September by Ena's
father, in his chauffeur-driven limousine, and promised a hearty
breakfast on the way, Andrea leaves Barcelona without having
achieved very much: 'Me marchaba sin haber conocido nada de lo
que confusamente esperaba: la vida en su plenitud, la alegría, el
interés profundo, el amor. De la casa de Aribau no me llevaba nada.
Al menos, así creía yo entonces' (294). Paradoxically, she now has
the possibility of fulfilling her desires and of moving up the social
ladder through no effort on her part whatsoever. *Nada* comes full
circle: Andrea's childhood dreams of reincorporation into a stable
bourgeois family are to be realized — or so it seems; the disruption
and threat symbolized by Aribau have been purged; a new
equilibrium is reached or more exactly there is a return to the status
quo, now represented by Ena's family. We thus have a happy ending,
typical of all the best romantic stories; yet, as before, Andrea's
chances for happiness and success arise not through her own
striving, but as a result of outside intervention. Ena's letter, like the
phone call before it, has a kind of providential function; it casts her
in the role of good fairy and Andrea as the unsuspecting Cinders

being called to the palace. However, in Andrea's case, if the past is any guide, moments of great expectation are usually short-lived and invariably followed by their opposite. So if *Nada* closes with Andrea's recovery of lost illusions in a new family setting, the chances are that disruption lurks around the corner — or has it already happened? Furthermore, if the novel is concerned with the emotional development of the main protagonist, little progress appears to have been made. Andrea seems to settle for the safety and intimacy of female companionship rather than take the further step into mature heterosexual relations.

3. *Character*

Since the publication of *Nada*, reviewers and critics have been fairly unanimous in their views on Laforet's character creations. Among the early reviewers, Ramón Descalzo, for example, saw them as 'personajes extraños y apasionantes'; José María de Cossío dubbed them as 'descentrados'; Manuel Fernández Almagro regarded the inhabitants of Aribau as agonized representatives of a bourgeoisie in crisis. More recently, Eugenio de Nora has referred to them as 'una galería de desequilibrados que, por rara casualidad, no sólo "andan sueltos", sino que están juntos (como pertenecientes a una misma familia)'.[2] Sanz Villanueva also remarks that *Nada*'s 'galería de anormalidades y excentricidades resulta excesiva, poco verosímil: demasiadas taras juntas para que los protagonistas resulten verdaderos' (p.295). The critics thus largely coincide in seeing Laforet's characters as abnormal, eccentric, neurotic, even pathological. More recently, the author has been taken to task for *Nada*'s lack of realism. Such a critique appears to operate on the assumption that Laforet set out to produce a realistic work and somehow went astray. Indeed, Sanz Villanueva refers to the novel's 'trasfondo documental' and its treatment of a 'tema intocable: la realidad inmediata' as signs of its commitment to realism (p. 296). But is this the case?

Let us remind ourselves that the novel is a retrospective account, an imaginative reconstruction, presented to the reader by the older Andrea. She is both protagonist and narrator, whose story constitutes a written version of the secret story of Aribau she desperately wished to reveal to Ena. This intention becomes redundant once Ena herself enters the story as an actor and begins to colonize a

---

[2] Descalzo, *Ya* (14 Aug.1945); Cossío, *Arriba* (15 Sept.1945); Fernández Almagro, *ABC* (13 Aug. 1945); Nora, *La novela española contemporánea*, III (Madrid, Gredos, 1970), pp.104-05.

world over whose secrets Andrea thought she had exclusive control. The novel, in a sense, comprises the very 'confidencias' Andrea wished to share with Ena, but which are now re-directed towards the reader. Given Andrea's inclinations towards literary invention, a passion which is amply recorded in the novel and even criticized by some of the characters (e.g. by Román, pp.38-39, and Ena, p.139), the highly fanciful, melodramatic and "literary" nature of *Nada* should not surprise us. Moreover, Andrea the narrator is trying to present an account of her experiences as a naive eighteen-year-old; consequently, her perceptions and interpretations of events are made to appear equivocal, indecisive and provisional. Logically, therefore, the written version of her story reflects all the vagaries, inconsistencies and gaps (intended or unintended) of her subjectivity. Also, as a result of the limitations of the first-person perspective on events, as well as the evasiveness which underpins the narrator's stance and her unwillingness to judge her characters, the story comes across as a very vague, mysterious and, in the end, unreliable account. As readers, therefore, we learn not to expect, nor are we given, a fully developed, logically consistent, realistic picture; the authority and credibility of the text are thus not secured. Indeed, the whole story might just as easily be a total fabrication, a product of Andrea's imagination, with little basis in lived experience. Of course, the novel is set in postwar Barcelona, a historically specific post-Civil-War Spanish reality. But, this reality is conveyed, not in a naturalistic or documentalist fashion, but in a highly subjective, imaginative manner. If we wished to categorise *Nada* in terms of realism we might loosely refer to the novel as a work of psychological realism or, as Feal Deibe describes it, 'realismo íntimo' (*12*, p.233). It is a realism which reveals how far the narrator has been seduced by the conventions of romantic fiction. For what we find portrayed in the novel is a black-and-white ethical world reminiscent of the fairy tale and fable in which the characters function as role models and represent opposing forces and desires. Far from being realistically presented ordinary people, they are larger than life, aberrations, distortions of the everyday, creatures taken to excess and deliberately so. Pattern seems to be far more important to Laforet than particularity. It would thus be mistaken to criticize the author too severely for her lack of realism, since this is not what she appears to be aiming for. Rather, it is romance, melodrama and the narrator's anxieties and unfulfilled ambitions which underpin the story and determine its highly dramatic mode of presentation.

In general, the characters in *Nada* are not presented as distinctive, highly individualized, complex figures, but as representatives of certain social, generational and class groupings and furthermore as projections of the narrator's fears and fantasies. The characters are her way of dramatizing those forces and impulses which both attract and repel her and which offer certain options for behaviour. In some cases, they represent desirable roles and positions she could not possibly occupy in real life, but whose potentialities she can externalize, gaze at and vicariously experience (e.g. Román and Ena); in other cases, they stand for roles she is being forced to occupy and to which she refuses to submit (e.g. Angustias). Overall, the characters are what she cannot be, but would like to be or what she is afraid of being; they represent her fears and wish fulfilments and these are put into motion through her fertile literary imagination.

The novel contains a wide spectrum of characters, including those who do not appear in the narrative, such as Andrea's cousin Isabel, Jerónimo Sanz's wife, Margarita's unnamed brother and of course those already dead, such as Andrea's grandfather and presumably her mother and father. But even if they do not appear, such characters none the less fulfil certain functions in the story. For example, Andrea's country cousin Isabel is one of several guardian figures in the novel, responsible for guaranteeing the propriety of her moral education and upbringing. However, she fails in this task and hands over the responsibility to Angustias. In terms of folktale morphology, for example, Isabel functions as the sender, the figure who arranges the protagonist's transfer to the city, to a more secure, controlled environment, under Angustias's watchful gaze. Isabel's action, which includes writing a letter to Angustias, also echoes Andrea's previous transfer from the convent to the village during wartime. It thus reinforces the journey motif in the novel and prefigures not only Angustias's own failure to impose on Andrea a traditional bourgeois education, but also Ena's letter of invitation to join her in Madrid. What is interesting is that Isabel's failure to discipline Andrea confirms Angustias's prejudices towards the paternal side of Andrea's family: 'la familia de tu padre ha sido siempre muy rara' (25). Here, then, a character who does not even appear fulfils a number of significant functions, which are repeated in the other female characters.

As regards the principal and secondary characters, they tend to be identified with particular settings. The two main settings are of course Aribau and Vía Layetana, which house the two contrasting families and symbolize a series of oppositions and divisions which operate throughout the novel. At Aribau, we find: the grandmother, the remaining members of her family (Román, Juan and Angustias), Juan's wife Gloria and their baby, Antonia the servant and various animals: a dog (Trueno), a cat and a parrot. If we include Andrea's mother Amalia and her two sisters, this makes a family of six children. There is also Jerónimo Sanz, Angustias's employer, ex-suitor and lover, who appears in Part 1. It may seem a little curious that the family at Aribau has virtually no contact with the neighbours or the caretaker and, if we discount Ena and her mother, no visitors except Sanz and, on the day of her departure for the convent, Angustias's friends. But life at Aribau is presented quite deliberately as a prison house, an enclosed space, cut off from the outside world: 'tan impenetrable a elementos extraños' (68), as Andrea reminds us. As regards Vía Layetana, we find a striking parallel with Aribau, again reminiscent of the symmetrical patterns often found in folk and fairy stories. The family of Vía Layetana is a numerically exact copy of Aribau. Luis and Margarita have produced six children, Ena and her five brothers, all of them blond. At Aribau, the grandparents have also produced six offspring, two brothers and four sisters, most of them dark. The contrast could not be clearer. Aribau represents the degenerate counterpart, the demonic inversion of the ideal family symbolized by Vía Layetana. The latter represents the new, modern, high-bourgeois household and from the narrator's point of view it is a post-war version of what Aribau might have been like during Andrea's childhood. Let us also remember that in Ena's family, although the grandmother is absent, the grandfather has survived the war, thus giving the family a degree of stability and continuity which is lacking at Aribau. In the latter case, the implication seems to be that the loss of the male head of household has led to a breakdown in order and discipline. Also, in a way reminiscent of Angustias's relationship with Sanz, Ena has a boy friend whom she cannot present to her family and for whom she has to conceal her feelings. This is Jaime, the 'señorito', friendly, patient, understanding, remarkably rich, but unsuited to the entrepreneurial mentality of Ena's family and thus unacceptable, at least until the end of the novel.

A further setting, but one which is not very frequently used, is the University. It functions as a meeting place for Andrea, Ena and their male student friends, including Gerardo and Pons. Compared to Aribau, the University (like Ena's house, where Andrea often studies) is an oasis, a refuge from the oppressions of Angustias and Aribau and a place where the youngsters can develop a sense of solidarity and resistance to the older generation. At the same time, since Ena usually pays for Andrea's drinks at the bar, the University is also the place where Andrea is made to feel economically inferior. The protagonist's sense of freedom is thus complemented by forms of oppression. From here, Andrea visits a further three connected settings. She accompanies Gerardo to the port area; she visits Pons's mansion, the scene of her abortive attempts at romance and the destruction of the Cinderella myth; she is also taken to the student flat in the *barrio gótico* (scene of her pursuit of Juan), inhabited by Pons's young intellectual friends, such as Yturdiaga, Guíxols and Pujol. The smugness, arrogance and wealth of opportunities of these upper-class youngsters are contrasted sharply with the poverty and lack of outlets endured by Juan, Aribau's inept, untalented, struggling artist, who is unable to feed his family. There is also a deliberate comparison made with Román's genuine artistic talent, which he has never successfully developed. The various linkages of place and contrasts of class and character are maintained, since the *barrio gótico* is also where Gloria's sister has her establishment and where Gloria earns money from gambling. So, in exploiting this traditionally dangerous and taboo location, Laforet emphasises a series of contrasts between lower, middle and upper class life-styles and opportunities.

Within these different settings, characters are grouped according to family, class and generation and are continually compared and contrasted. Reflecting the novel's clear binary divisions, the characters dramatize the collision and fearful inter-mingling of two opposed worlds, symbolised by Aribau and Vía Layetana. And let us recall that this blurring of the boundaries and mixing of worlds have already occurred in the past. The characters thus function as agents and vehicles for this renewed clash of differ-ences. They re-stage past conflicts and past scenes of desire and in the process illustrate, among other things: the economic and psychological collapse of Spain's traditional bourgeoisie after the civil war; the conflict between generations and classes and the destabilizing effects of unregulated male, and also female, sexuality.

The process of characterization in *Nada* is somewhat problem-atic, not only in terms of the author's handling of character construc-tion, but also regarding the question of identity. One of the crucial, distinguishing features of character identity is, of course, a name, and in Laforet's novel naming is by no means a clear and straight-forward matter. Indeed, Laforet adopts different modes of character identification: some are known only by their first names (Román, Juan, Ena, Angustias, Gloria, Gerardo, Jaime, Antonia); others by their surnames (Sanz, Pons, Pujol, Yturdiaga, Guíxols); others by the generic group to which they belong (Andrea's 'abuelos', Ena's 'hermanos'); other character names are deeply embedded in the text and rarely mentioned (Amalia, Andrea's mother, Margarita and Luis, Ena's parents); other names are simply left undisclosed (those of Andrea's father, Gloria's sister, Sanz's wife, Margarita's brother, the 'abuelos' of both families). From this, we might infer that naming is largely a function of the preferences and attitudes of the narrator of the story, whose own uncertainties and confusions emerge in this jumbled hodgepodge of different naming conventions. None the less, certain distinctions can be made. For example, the narrator seems to use first names for relatively major characters and those closest to her and surnames for minor or secondary characters, although in the case of Pons this rule breaks down, given his importance as Andrea's potential Prince Charming at the end of Part II. Also, certain names are peculiarly appropriate for the character they identify and carry a powerful emotional charge for the narrator: Angustias (anguish, anxiety, repression); Gloria (beautiful, wild, sensual, unrestrained, as compared to Angustias); Román (romantic, romance, sexual attraction, source of mature experience); it is all the more curious therefore, why the hideous Antonia is not given a more graphic, suggestive name. Naming in *Nada* appears to be a rag-bag but what is striking is that the surnames of the two main families are withheld. We never learn the surname of Ena's family and even when Angustias assures Andrea that 'ahora tienes una familia, un hogar y un nombre' (58), the latter is not divulged. About all we know of Andrea's name, as Ena points out, is that she has the same 'segundo apellido, tan extraño' (61), as Román. All of this suggests a powerful reluctance, if not a refusal, on the part of the narrator to fully identify the main families, in a novel where the family and its role are crucial. By refusing to do so, Laforet may be indicating that the existence and indeed the achievement of a secure, stable family identity in *Nada* remain problematic.

Although Laforet's characters are not fully realized, they are given certain distinguishing features. Apart from proper names, a further mode of presenting them is found in the widespread use of animal metaphors. These tend to be extremely familiar and conventional, as one might expect from an inexperienced twenty-two-year-old novelist. But as Kathleen Glenn suggests in her detailed study of this aspect of the novel, they provide Laforet with a shorthand means of indicating character traits, behaviour and roles (*15*). For example, the grandmother is compared to an 'animalillo' (18); the use of the diminutive obviously suggests her physical smallness, but it also evokes her frailty and helplessness. Gloria is often referred to by Angustias as a 'serpiente', the agent of evil which has corrupted paradise and caused the downfall of Aribau. Yet Gloria is hardly the sly, cunning figure evoked by the word 'serpiente' or the menacing, treacherous creature of Angustias' fantasy. Indeed, when Andrea refers to her and observes that: 'la mujer serpiente durmió enroscada'

(104), it is in a humorous and ironic way. This suggests that the threat represented by Gloria is imaginary and that she takes on the role of scapegoat for Angustias's frustrations and repressions. Román has a strange power to evoke devotion and dependence in others and this trait is suggested in the comparison of his victims with dogs. For the rest of the family of Aribau, Antonia is a 'fiera' (52), but for Román she is totally identified with his dog Trueno and her devotion to the master is equally dog-like. In similar fashion, Juan is compared to a dog during his descent into the *barrio chino* (179) and after Román's suicide, to which he reacts with 'gemidos desesperados' (293). The relationships between Juan and Gloria and Román and Ena are often described in terms of a cat-and-mouse game, the inhabitants of Aribau are seen by Román as rats on a sinking ship, Angustias's friends are compared to crows, Aribau itself is animalized, emitting groans and smells. On the whole, as Glenn suggests in her study, the animal imagery is simple and even clichéd; it helps to evoke vivid mental pictures of character behaviour and a general mood of degeneracy and decay. With regard to Aribau, this is enhanced through the appearance of the various domestic animals who reflect, in their wasted and diseased state, the condition of the house and its inhabitants. Furthermore, animal imagery allows Laforet to draw a line between what is normal and abnormal, what is socially acceptable and unacceptable. That is, it allows her to define and deflect the 'other', to neutralize the threat of unruly passions or behaviour. For example, when Gloria, in conversation with Andrea, accuses Ena of being 'la amante de Román', Andrea responds angrily: 'Eres como un animal [...] Tú y Juan sois como bestias. ¿Es que no cabe otra cosa entre un hombre y una mujer? ¿Es que no concibes nada más en el amor? ¡Oh! ¡Sucia!' (252). Andrea is driven to defend her friend from any imputation of contact and involvement with Román, by which she might be tarnished as a loose woman and open to sexual desire. Put another way, Andrea feels compelled to uphold Ena's virtue and purity since her own identity is so bound up with that of her best friend. Animality and dirt, which encapsulate the atmosphere of Aribau, are thus two of the negative categories Andrea will employ to keep at a distance the threat of mature sexual relations, which she regards as bestial and degrading. She will insist on the purity and un-sexed nature of female characters, like Ena, and until the disaster at Pons's ball, will uphold a naive notion of unsullied romantic love.

Another way in which Laforet presents her characters is through their appearance. To the narrator and through her to the reader, physical qualities and distinctive bodily features are all-important. Indeed, characterisation in *Nada* in general is developed through the physical features of the players, particularly their faces. The grandmother for example, is described as a 'viejecita decrépita' (14), yet she is identified by Andrea because of her 'sonrisa de bondad tan dulce' (44). Juan is described as a lugubrious, emaciated figure, 'un tipo descarnado y alto' and one with 'la cara llena de concavidades como una calavera' (14); Antonia 'parecía horrible y destrozada' (15), revealing 'la verdosa dentadura que me sonreía' (15). Gloria is recognised by her 'cabellos revueltos y rojizos' (15), her 'aguda cara blanca' and seen as a 'despeinada, mujer desgreñada' (16). Angustias has 'cabellos entrecanos', but also reveals 'cierta belleza en su cara oscura y estrecha' (15). The narrator seems keen to show that for the young Andrea, first impressions of physical presence are powerful and lasting, and even in the authoritarian Angustias, Andrea can find beauty, a 'gran belleza de líneas' (27). Andrea's initial description of Ena is very similar: 'una agradable y sensual cara en la que relucían unos ojos terribles' (60). The narrator attempts, therefore, to bring out both the unattractive and also the attractive features of the characters' physical make-up and the paradoxical co-existence of attraction and repulsion, beauty and menace, in the same figure. If Andrea is made to feel threatened or guilty by another character, one of the ways she has of alleviating her anxiety is to light on a negative physical trait; this is perhaps reminiscent of the way children cope with adults who appear threatening. For example, feeling particularly oppressed by Angustias, Andrea tells us, 'le buscaba un detalle repugnante' (27), that is, her 'dientes de un color sucio' (28). Fearful of Antonia, Andrea singles out her 'fea cara' and her 'mueca desafiante, como de triunfo' (31). Interestingly, the narrator recognizes the equivocal and unreliable nature of first impressions and appearances when talking of Angustias: 'Y la juzgaba, sin ninguna compasión, corta de luces y autoritaria. He hecho tantos juicios equivocados en mi vida, que aun no sé si éste era verdadero' (27). This point links up with a more general feature of character behaviour: that of taking appearances at face value and in stubbornly keeping up appearances, even in the face of contrary evidence. One of the lessons we are meant to draw from *Nada* is that appearances are fundamentally important but highly deceptive, since they conceal many layers of meaning and behaviour which are attractive but also potentially threatening. Also, the concern with appearances is bound up with an intense interest, even an obsession with the physical form of the human body, particularly where this is related to the potential for sensuality or eroticism. Andrea in the shower, Gloria posing nude, the nude statue in the park, are just some of the instances which reveal the protagonist's ambivalent attitude towards female sensuality. Moreover, a number of the references to water and its purging, cleansing effects relate precisely to the protagonist's difficulty of coping with being seen as a sensual woman. After Juan accuses her of being: '...Cargada de amantes, suelta por Barcelona como un perro...' (199), Andrea takes to the shower, but without gaining relief and metaphorically without cleansing herself of the stain of her imagined lasciviousness: 'El agua, que se volcaba sobre mi cuerpo me parecía tibia, incapaz de refrescar mi carne ni de limpiarla' (199-200).

Turning now to a more detailed consideration of the main characters, the grandmother is the first character to meet Andrea on her arrival at Aribau. She is initially perceived by the protagonist not as a solid human being but as 'la mancha blanquinegra de una viejecita decrépita' (13), a shadowy, ghostly figure. The incorporeality and other-worldliness of the grandmother are reinforced by the fact that she rarely sleeps but, like Antonia the servant, wanders the house at night (52). This adds significantly to Andrea's imaginative view of Aribau as some sort of decaying Gothic mansion populated by the living dead. (In an equally Gothic vein, after his suicide, Andrea refers to Román in life as 'el espectro de un muerto' (280), who finally returns to the grave.) The grandmother's misrecognition of Andrea at the door (taking her to be Gloria returning from her nocturnal activities because of the late hour) is significant. It partly exposes her senility but it also makes Andrea — and through her the reader — extremely 'intrigada' (14) regarding the secrets of the house and Gloria's own story, with which Andrea's has many important parallels. The grandmother initially represents Aribau's extreme degradation, its physical and moral collapse. Yet it was not always like this. Andrea notices on the wall a portrait of her grandparents in their prime: the grandfather 'muy guapo, con la espesa barba castaña' (21), with the grandmother dutifully and demurely smiling behind him; the contrast with 'la pequeña momia irreconocible' (23) of the previous night could not be more striking. The picture represents an admittedly idealized portrait of the vitality and self-confidence of traditional patriarchal society and also reinforces the fact of the shattering transformation that has overtaken Aribau since the Civil War. Now the *abuela* takes refuge from loneliness and despair in religion and prayer. Unlike Angustias, who has no true vocation for the spiritual life, the grandmother reveals a genuine devotion. She speaks to God and the Virgin (106) and, according to Gloria, such spirituality makes her better able to understand others and forgive them. Moreover, the grandmother consistently refers to her compassion and support for the underdog and the oppressed. She always defends Gloria from Angustias's accusations and Juan's temper. She also instinctively defends her two sons, even when they least deserve it (as happens when Gloria fears that Juan might kill her because of his grief at his brother's death, 291). However, this kindly old woman was not always such a saint. Indeed, through the grandmother, Laforet mounts a critique of a particular conception of family upbringing and motherhood, based on a re-examination of the past. In its heyday, family life at Aribau was organized according to a double standard: Angustias refers to the fact that the boys were over-indulged and allowed to run riot whilst the girls were subjected to the strictest controls in dress, behaviour and activities (95). In this process, the grandmother played the role of the authoritarian mother, being incapable of controlling the boys and thus overcompensating by punishing the girls. This model of parenting is held up at the end of the novel as the fundamental cause of family breakdown and Román's suicide: 'Siempre fue usted injusta, mamá', remarks one of the sisters, 'Siempre prefirió usted a sus hijos varones. ¿Se da usted cuenta de que tiene usted la culpa de este final?' (283). Also, evidence of the grandmother's attitude towards physical and sexual contact in her younger days has disturbing parallels with Andrea's experiences with men, especially with Gerardo. She reveals to Andrea: '...Tu abuelo me dio una vez un beso... Yo no se lo perdoné en muchos años' (47). The implication seems to be that such repressions and self-denial are handed down from generation to generation. Overall, despite her senility and helplessness, the grandmother comes across as a kindly, protective though ineffectual figure. In the past, however, this was accompanied by a mode of upbringing which blighted the emotional development of her sons and especially that of her daughters.

Angustias is the only one of the grandmother's four daughters to have remained in the family at Aribau without marrying. An embittered, middle-aged spinster, she represents an extreme version of the traditional 'beata', who tries to repress in others what she has been deprived of herself. Like the grandmother, she is an unsuccessful mother figure, as she readily admits to Andrea (102). Indeed, in her role as Andrea's guardian, she becomes her jailer, keeping her under surveillance on her outings in the city and feeling scandalized that, on her arrival, Andrea made the journey from the station to Aribau alone (25). Her room, which reflects the austerity of the convent cell, is likened to a gigantic ear, open to all the sounds and whispers emanating from the house and its staircase (87). Angustias is evidently the tragic victim of a repressive and rigidly organized female education. As Román points out (40), her sisters have all married the first eligible men to come along, simply to escape the restrictions of family life at Aribau. Ironically, perhaps, Angustias has observed the tradition of courtship but her choice of Jerónimo Sanz, the son of a shopkeeper (110), was not acceptable to her father because of his lowly social and economic position. Denied her choice in love and incapable of breaking out of her dependency on the family, Angustias became a slave to paternal dictates. In many

ways, she sacrifices her own emotional fulfilment and happiness for
the sake of maintaining patriarchal and class differences. She has
been made to serve the needs of male-defined family norms and, to
justify and compensate for her sacrifice, she adopts an inflated sense
of her own superiority and indispensability, as the mainstay of the
family. Not surprisingly, when her father dies, she assumes the
mantle of patriarchal values and becomes the surrogate master of the
house, projecting onto her new, adoptive daughter (Andrea) the
resentments, repressions and denials wreaked upon her as an adolescent. These are particularly severe in relation to sexual instincts and
the body, which she regards as supremely sinful and to be punished.
It is no surprise, then, that when Gloria enters Aribau at the end of
the war, Angustias regards her as a fallen woman, evil incarnate and
a class enemy. Nor is it totally unexpected when Angustias finally
takes the road to total self-abnegation of desire and the body by
becoming a nun. This happens even though she has absolutely no
vocation and is the result of her continuing secret affair with Sanz.
Angustias no doubt still loves and desires Sanz (now a married man
whose wife, because of this lingering affair, has gone mad), but she
cannot let that love be known. It conflicts with her duty towards
Aribau and her view of herself as virtuous and unsullied by unruly
passions. Unable to cope any longer with the stress of her double life
and having failed to domesticate Andrea, she finds escape in another
type of imprisonment. Her self-imposed exile in a convent is yet
another example of her deeply masochistic nature; by imprisoning
herself, she asserts an identity based on pain and suffering and the
repression of desire. To guard against such temptations, as Angustias
advises Andrea, a girl must become a fortress (25). The notion of
fortress is perhaps one of the key metaphors used in relation to
female sexuality and gender roles in the novel and which, as
previously noted, finds direct expression in Angustias's 'dos únicos
caminos honrosos' (101) for women, i.e. marriage or the convent.
Unless women are protected by these institutions, the argument
seems to be, then disaster is bound to follow. Indeed, Angustias
predicts disaster for Andrea, seeing her as incapable of controlling
her desires: 'Tú no dominarás tu cuerpo y tu alma. Tú no, tú no... Tú

no podrás dominarlos' (103). Paradoxically, in this bitter, neurotic, masochistic defender of archaic Spain, Andrea finds much to admire, including her moral rectitude (99). Moreover, Andrea will absorb far more from her aunt's example than she realizes, gradually building up her defences against desire.

Compared to Angustias, Gloria represents freedom, openness and a total lack of inhibitions. As her name suggests, she glorifies in her own girlish attractiveness, which, at least initially, Andrea finds off-putting (15). This is clearly not how young mothers or for that matter well-brought-up women of a certain class, like Andrea, are meant to behave. But in other ways, Andrea is seduced by Gloria's naive naturalness, physicality and sensuality, which first emerged the day she saw her posing nude for Juan: 'aparecía increíblemente bella y blanca entre la fealdad de todas las cosas, como un milagro del Señor' (36). As long as the body is located in a socially acceptable, culturally legitimized context (e.g. painting, sculpture, religion), Andrea seems able to respond to it in a sensual manner. While Angustias regards the body not only as a site of sin and evil, but also as something not to be displayed, something alien from her which belongs to her father, as the guardian of her class, Gloria luxuriates in her own body and feels no qualms in boasting of her own physical attraction. According to Andrea (35), Gloria is not very intelligent but, in certain respects, she fulfils the youngster's ideal of femininity. After initially viewing her as stupid and slovenly, Andrea changes her view and notes in her: 'Una inteligencia sutil y diluida en la cálida superficie de la piel perfecta' (36). It is clear that Andrea feels attracted to Gloria, who functions as a projection of her own very suggestible, responsive sensuality. The two women share a desire to escape the lugubrious atmosphere of Aribau, Andrea through her walks in the city and Gloria through her secret, nocturnal outings to her sister's bar in the *barrio gótico*. Both of them also coincide on the stairs which lead up to Román's flat. Here, Andrea repeats Gloria's tendency to spy on Román (a trait which derives, according to the grandmother, from the fact that both are orphans, 50). Also, Gloria's earlier infatuation and affair with the dark prince is recycled through Andrea. This time, however, it is music, not painting, which breaches Andrea's defences, acts as the hypnotic agent and renders her vulnerable to Román's seductive advances.

As noted earlier, Andrea is intrigued by Gloria from the very start, particularly over whether — as Román continually insinuates — she is a loose woman and secretly involved in some form of prostitution. By following Juan into the *barrio gótico* on a mission to save Gloria, Andrea is able to confirm that, despite the outward signs (it is late, the baby is ill, Gloria has put on her best dress and is heavily made up), she is not selling her body; according to her sister, however, she could easily do so (181). In fact, far from being the supposedly lascivious woman and unfaithful wife which Andrea imagines, Gloria has been hard at work supporting her husband and baby by gambling. She has combined her need for an outlet from Aribau with an unusual though profitable occupation: 'Es la única manera de tener un poco de dinero honradamente' (246), she tells Andrea. Gloria is thus engaged in honest labour, apart from which the work can be exciting: 'Es muy emocionante jugar, chica' (246). So, far from betraying her husband and abandoning her baby, she is in fact combining the traditional, supportive roles of wife and mother with that of breadwinner. Her sister acerbically points out to Juan the main purpose of such apparently questionable activity: 'Todo para que el señorón se crea que es un pintor famoso' (181). Gloria is even selling Juan's worthless paintings to the 'traperos' in order to make ends meet, though this is of course done secretly. Thus despite her outward image, her need for 'esparcimiento', Román's insinuations and Andrea's fantasies, Gloria is at bottom a dutiful servant of the patriarchal family, indeed she is its economic mainstay. In a sense, the crisis-ridden bourgeoisie of Aribau, in a clearly parasitic fashion, are surviving largely by the labours of the lower orders, including Antonia as well as Gloria. However, Juan refuses to accept his wife's role as a working mother; in view of his brother's jibes and his own sense of failure as a husband, it is too much of a threat to his own precarious position as family head. Thus his insecurities are easily exploited by Román and as a way of channelling his rage he frequently beats his wife. At one point, after a particularly severe drubbing and a soaking, Gloria takes refuge in bed with Andrea.

Here, Andrea expresses a desire to bite her: 'Algo así como una locura se posesionó de mi bestialidad al sentir tan cerca el latido de aquel cuello de Gloria... Ganas de morder en la carne palpitante, masticar. Tragar la buena sangre tibia...' (132). Such an unusual desire can hardly be rationally explained by Andrea's hunger, of which she constantly complains. Apart from the echoes of Gothic vampirism, it is also suggestive of a fantasy in which Andrea wishes to penetrate and merge with a protective figure. Gloria perhaps functions here for Andrea as a mother substitute, a role that is also played by the grandmother, Margarita and also Ena. These are all characters in whom Andrea, at one time or another, seeks refuge and maternal protection and expresses a desire to fuse, to blur the boundaries of self and other; in short, to regress to infancy and become 'nada'.

Later in the novel, Andrea spies on an encounter in the street outside the flat between Román and Gloria, whom he tries to seduce by reminding her of their affair at the castle during the war. This scene has already appeared in one of Andrea's dreams, where she projects onto Gloria the attributes of the sinful woman. However, in this meeting, which is continued inside the house, Gloria refuses to be swayed. Indeed, her words prefigure Román's grisly end: 'Te quiero igual que al cerdo que se lleva al matadero' (205). All that can be proved is that Gloria was genuinely in love with Román before marrying Juan and was prepared to give herself to him, but her love was not returned. Indeed, Román simply humiliated her in front of his friends. She further reveals that she betrayed him to the police during the war and would do it again (207). Gloria is thus a character of considerable fortitude and resolve. And despite the fact she is still attracted to him, she is able to withstand his advances. Her image as the unfaithful, whorish, sensual woman corresponds not so much to her own actions but to the distorted views of others, including those of Andrea. At the end of the novel, and having again taken revenge on Román by reporting him for his black-market activities, Gloria sees herself as responsible for his death (280). Not surprisingly, she feels extremely afraid of Juan, who reacts violently to his brother's death by beating her again and wishing to kill her (291). Fearing for her own safety and that of the baby, she concludes that the only place for Juan is the lunatic asylum, a view strongly resisted by the grandmother (291), still unwilling to acknowledge the evidence of Juan's psychological break-down. Gloria emerges, then, as a victim of Juan's easily-provoked cruelty and, by implication, of his homo-erotic relationship with his brother Román. In a sense, she has projected onto her the frustration and rage of the brothers, who have difficulties in sustaining conventional heterosexual attachments. Gloria is also a victim of a class system which regards her as an inferior and of a reactionary morality which feels threatened by the vitality and uninhibited sensuality she exudes. Above all, while on the surface Gloria gives the impression of being a dangerous, lascivious, sinful creature, she is in fact a model of motherhood and self-abnegation, besides being the economic foundation of the family. And, like the other supposedly tainted women of the novel, she emerges as totally redeemed. Her case helps to reinforce the grandmother's warning that 'no todas las cosas que se ven son lo que parecen' (83).

Juan is a volatile, unpredictable figure, caught in a tangled web of insecurities, contradictions and failures. He is dogged by an inferiority complex and a slavish dependence on his handsome, multi-talented brother. Indeed, Román represents for Juan what Ena represents for Andrea: a wish-fulfilment, an ego-ideal, a figure in whom all lacks and desires are invested. Since childhood, Juan has always been less successful and talented than his brother but has always been prepared to support Román, even when the latter has not reciprocated. It also appears that Juan's sensitive character and early artistic leanings were regarded by his father as unmanly. Unable to fulfil his father's expectations, he has spent considerable time in the Foreign Legion (an escape much like Angustias's escape to the convent, but in Juan's case, a way of purging the feminine side of his character and asserting his male identity). He has none the less maintained his interest in art and bought paintings. On the death of his father, he has taken over his office and transformed it into a studio. Also, though acutely aware of his class origins and bourgeois status, Juan has married Gloria after a passionate, lightning romance.

Being a man, however, has allowed him to do what Angustias was prevented from doing, i.e. marry someone from an inferior social class. At the same time, this has engendered powerful resentments and envy not only in Angustias, but in Román (with whom Gloria had an affair) and Antonia (in love with Román and bitterly jealous of Gloria). So, apart from failing to live up to paternal expectations, Juan has transgressed family and class boundaries by introducing an outsider into Aribau, upon whom other family members heap their prejudices and frustrations. Because he is unable to resolve these contradictions and finds himself in a constant state of tension, Juan can be extremely aggressive and his anger easily provoked. He is open to violent swings of mood and forced into asserting a male authority that his tortured, fragmentary identity tends to negate. Occasionally he can be very loving and attentive, as Gloria tells us (53). Unfortunately, he is unable to keep his wife and baby. His badly paid job as a night watchman is a threat to his self-esteem and is a constant source of embarrassment, revealing how the bourgeoisie of Aribau have been reduced to engaging in manual labour. Also, because of a lack of talent, he is unable to paint good pictures, unlike Román who (though no less a failure in other ways) finds it almost effortless. As a result, Juan ends up producing abysmal nude portraits of his wife, who then proceeds to sell them off cheaply to the 'traperos'. Juan's work may not be the high art to which he evidently aspires, but thanks to Gloria's ingenuity it is put to good use: it is commercialized and provides a small return. In another sense, Juan is unwittingly engaged in what might have passed in 1940s Spain for the pornography trade, and ironically it is Gloria, his wife and model, whose fine sensuous body is a major source of their income. However, Juan is unable to come to terms with the idea that his wife might actually be keeping him; this reversal of roles represents a powerful threat to traditional notions of masculinity and gender stereotypes which, in Juan's case, are already in crisis.

As noted earlier, Juan is the victim of Román's constant sniping and provocations concerning Gloria's fidelity. Confronted by his own weakness and lack of correspondence to the required patriarchal norm, he is continually pressed to assert the crudest and most objectionable forms of male power, including that of wife-beating. For his part, Román is engaged in an almost constant guerrilla war against Gloria, trying to provoke and humiliate her and, when not able to do so directly, he exploits his brother, over whom he wields an almost god-like power. Juan is thus Román's slave, his dog (just like Antonia), and finds himself trapped in a relation of total dependence to a point where he has no will or reasoning of his own. Yet, as a counterweight to his violent rages and ugly moods, Juan appears to be a devoted father to his child; how else can we explain his decision to take part-time work? But he is unable to contemplate the idea of Gloria functioning as a working mother; indeed, the whole notion of the mother working outside the home is given negative connotations and associated with prostitution. In general, like Angustias, Juan has suffered two major developmental traumas. Firstly, he has been the victim of a doting, indulgent mother and a cold, distant, authoritarian father. Secondly, he has been denied self-confidence and a secure identity by a cruel, castrating brother, to whom he has become emotionally attached. And one suspects that his own inner turmoil is largely the result of his contradictory sexuality. He loves his wife and child, but his feelings for his brother seem even more powerful, indicating a latent homosexuality which cannot find an outlet and which expresses itself in violent, neurotic behaviour. This is so after Román's suicide, when in his grief and rage at the death of his tormentor, he threatens to kill Gloria, still egged on by his brother: 'Dice que Román se le aparece todas las noches para aconsejarle que me mate' (290). Román continues to exercise power over his brother even from beyond the grave.

As the name suggests, Román is a composite figure, one in which Laforet invests her rather stereotyped notions of the decadent romantic hero. She also uses the character to represent the more dangerous and threatening side of male sexuality. Unmarried, a double agent during the war and now involved in black marketeering, Román is a lone wolf, an opportunist, and has adapted well to postwar conditions. He can afford new clothes and always seems to have ample supplies of scarce items, such as coffee and cigarettes. Before he appears, Angustias warns Andrea of his violent, sadistic behaviour. This, she surmises, is the outcome of his traumatic experience in a Republican prison during the war (27). Román is thus a victim of what the winning side in the Civil War constantly referred to as 'el terror rojo'. It also emerges that Román lives apart from the rest of the family in an upstairs flat — an oasis of relative order, as Andrea discovers, much like Angustias' room. From his lofty vantage point, he makes regular forays into the flat below, a world he despises. Indeed, it is as if he were driven by an inner compulsion to return to this very scene, to rummage, investigate, survey and expose the activities and secrets of Aribau. Like Andrea, he is a compulsive observer of others, allowing nothing to escape his powerful gaze. When we first meet him, he is cast in the mould of the dark, charismatic, romantic hero: 'con el pelo rizado y la cara agradable e inteligente' (28); animals have an instinctive liking for him (28) and Andrea is immediately drawn to him by his 'exuberancia afectuosa' (28); he is also seen greasing a pistol. This rather conventional, clichéd signifier (which emerges later, in Andrea's imagination, when she tries to rescue Ena from Román's clutches) immediately presents Román as an unconventional, potentially threatening figure. The fact that the possession of guns is illegal situates him on the border between legality and criminality. This initial impression is complemented by his violent swings of mood and his attempts to provoke his brother into hitting Gloria. Already, we have an inkling of the master-slave relationship between the two brothers and signs of the sadistic way in which Román relates to other members of the family.

Despite warnings from Angustias and Gloria (37), Andrea finds herself strongly attracted to Román; she is particularly drawn to his body, especially the 'agilidad enorme en su delgado cuerpo' (39), the 'muelles bajo los músculos morenos' (40), his hands 'llenas de vida' (40). Though middle-aged, Román is still exceptionally handsome and comes to symbolize a mature prince, a worldly-wise warrior, a figure embodying the essence of patriarchal energy. Inevitably, as in the cases of Margarita and Gloria, Andrea is smitten by the dark hero, seduced not least by his artistic talents and in particular by his skill on the violin. Román's music penetrates to her depths and has the effect of dissolving her emotional defenses: 'Mi alma [...] recibía el sonido como una lluvia la tierra áspera' (41). Here, faced with Andrea's swooning response, Román believes he has found a soul-mate in her, a confirmation of himself, a reflection in the mirror. And having read Isabel's letter (in which he presumably learns of Andrea's bad behaviour while living with her cousin), he takes the youngster to be someone who will understand him and match his own perversity and cruelty. Afraid to disillusion her uncle and reveal her own sentimental ordinariness, Andrea tries to keep up appearances and to play the role of the sophisticated female. She is undoubtedly attracted by her uncle but he makes her feel inferior and fearful and she intuits that she might become yet another of his conquests. It will be left to Ena to fulfil the role of the strong female and she will do so with the sort of panache and consummate style Andrea can only fantasize about. Moreover, it is not equality Román yearns for, but the power to control and dominate. Significantly, he remarks to Andrea: 'A ti se te podría hipnotizar' (41), recognizing her suggestibility, her desire for escape and the ease with which she might be controlled. In fact, Andrea's apparent ecstasy somewhat disconcerts him since he is not at all interested in women who give in too easily and deprive him of a struggle. For Román, the stronger the woman, the more exciting and challenging the seduction process becomes. He is thus portrayed as the demonic artist/creator, the Svengali, the manipulator of others. He is the master craftsman, the sculptor of idols and false gods, and in Xochipilli, his Aztec deity, he has fabricated a totem of cruelty and sacrifice in his own image. In a sense, he has given physical form to his own towering ego and sees himself as a god. He is a savage god, however, one that controls others, demands sacrifices and gloats over their subjection. As he says of Juan to Andrea: 'Tú sabes muy bien hasta qué punto Juan me pertenece, hasta qué punto se arrastra tras de mí, hasta qué punto le maltrato [...] Yo le dejo así, que se hunda solo... Y los demás...Y a toda la familia de la casa, sucia como un río revuelto' (91). Román is also a recluse, he lives alone, upstairs, in hiding almost (67) and has

no friends. He is disparaging about Andrea's 'romanticismo de
colegiala por las amistades' (89); he has no genuine feelings for
anyone but himself. It is only the suffering he causes others which
engages him and stimulates his interest. So, despite his many talents,
Román is a total failure as a human being. Even his outward
demeanour as a romantic hero is belied by his introversion and self-
loathing: 'Yo creo que he perdido el gusto por lo colosal. El tictac de
mis relojes me despierta los sentidos más que el viento en los
desfiladeros... Yo estoy cerrado' (66-67).

Apart from his artistic talents, Román's power over others
seems to reside in his charisma and especially in his sexual
knowledge. He is portrayed as the gatekeeper to the forbidden, the
source of mature adult experience in the arts of love and sex. He is
thus highly attractive but also highly repellent to Andrea. Yet his
maturity is something of a mirage. His sexual knowledge is not made
clear (as far as we know, he has never managed to form a lasting
relationship, nor has he ever made love to anyone). He also behaves
in a totally narcissistic way, acting like the eternal child, constantly
seeking to assert his control and omnipotence. He has already
exploited other women. For example, Margarita, Ena's mother,
blindly gave in to him by sacrificing her beautiful, flowing 'trenza'
(235), thereby symbolically mutilating herself for him. Gloria also
allowed herself to be painted nude, but only to be ridiculed by
Román's army friends, and once installed at Aribau, became the
victim of his cruelty through his slave and double, Juan. Andrea
finally realizes the violent, aggressive nature of Román's character
after the incident of the scarf, the theft of which he tries to blame on
Gloria. Yet, despite such evidence, the grandmother and Juan refuse
to recognise Román's evil streak; it is left to the latest in the line of
the dark hero's female consorts, Ena, to reverse the process and
avenge male brutality and violence.

As in Juan's case, the source of Román's disturbance can be
traced back to the grandmother and to a particular mode of family
upbringing. As Gloria suggests, referring to the grandmother: 'Pues,
Román no la quiere a usted, mamá; dice que los ha hecho
desgraciados a todos con su procedimiento' (45). Here, Gloria refers

to the grandmother's double standard: the severe control and repression of her daughters, compared to the indulgence heaped upon her sons which eventually leads to Román's suicide: 'ahí, tienes el pago de los varones' remarks one of the daughters, 'de los que tú mimabas' (283). An excess of motherly love is thus adduced as a major cause of Aribau's problems. Indeed, this is indicated in the fact that Román is unable to leave Aribau, unable to totally separate himself from the family space and, symbolically, from the maternal breast. On the outside, Román is portrayed as conventionally masculine (he is athletic, sexually attractive, charismatic); on the inside, however, he is ambiguous, if not ambivalent, in terms of his sexual identity. In a sense, he has suffered because of women (he is a victim of his mother's 'mimo' and Gloria's denunciation, which landed him in a Republican jail), although he has also been saved by them (by Antonia for example who, because of her love for him, spoke up in his favour to the authorities and had him released from prison; yet, as his class inferior, she has to be content with possessing a substitute, i.e. his dog and not him). Despite Andrea's observation that Román is a 'fondo inagotable de posibilidades' (41) and potentially a great artist, he himself recognizes his own fundamental lack of worth: 'Juan y yo, que somos dos canallas' (40). Indeed, he indulges himself in trying to steal his sisters' birthright, disrupt his brother's marriage and pervert the innocence of young women. His project, if we can use that term, seems to have at its source the destruction of patriarchy and the traditional family. Like Ena to a large extent, Román projects onto the world the mistakes and problems of a traditional pattern of upbringing and wreaks his revenge.

Overall, Román is a male figure onto which a young female writer (Laforet) has projected her fears and anxieties about her own sex. As mentioned earlier, he is a composite of a satanic monster, a demonic child but also a rebellious female, who sets out to overturn a type of family, marriage and society which have distorted and destroyed him. He is anxious to find a partner, he wants someone to talk to, to understand and appreciate his talents, but he simply cannot overcome his infantile cruelty. He thus projects onto women the perceived hurt done to him. He is highly cultured, but also exceedingly raw. One of the purposes of Laforet's novel will be to cook Román's rawness, his literal crudity, and through his humiliation by Ena and eventual suicide, he will become metaphorically cleansed and purified. His energy, his power to attract and seduce, will be exorcised and traditional patriarchal relations will be restored. As in all those stories where elemental human energies and passions are counterposed to civilized society, passion always fails. Nature, as represented by Román, will be overcome by Culture. Marriage, children and family life will inevitably triumph over the destabilizing influence of a perverted male sexuality.

Andrea, as we have seen, finds escape from the oppressive, though fascinating, atmosphere of Aribau in her University friends. It is only her female rather than her male friends, however, who are able to satisfy her need for intimacy, gossip and her desire to confide the story of Aribau: 'Comprendí en seguida que con los muchachos era imposible el tono misterioso y reticente de las confidencias, al que las chicas suelen ser aficionadas, el encanto de desmenuzar el alma, el roce de la sensibilidad almacenada durante años...' (59). She thus gravitates towards Ena, whom she wishes to adopt as her confidante and who also fulfils, to some extent, a maternal function. Ena's mother, Margarita, will also embody this role, but as the good mother figure in contrast to Angustias, who represents the bad mother. Ena, as we have already seen, belongs to an apparently stable, progressive, caring, high-bourgeois family. And in Andrea's first encounter with her, as was the case with Román, Andrea finds herself physically attracted, strongly drawn by the other's 'agradable y sensual cara' (60). At the same time, she is slightly perturbed by Ena's 'ojos terribles' (60) and already aware of other telling features: 'Su malicia y su inteligencia eran proverbiales' (60). Again, as in the case of Román, Ena is a mixture of the attractive and the repellent, of protectiveness and threat; and at least in public, she personifies the self-confident, but also cruel and malevolent, female. She is thus a clear and direct counterpart to Román, his female equivalent, a figure who embodies a number of features found in the predatory male. Moreover, she represents everything that Andrea is not: 'Me hizo sentirme todo lo que no era: rica y feliz' (70). As previously

mentioned, Ena is Andrea's ego ideal, the fulfilment of all her
fantasies regarding female power and social superiority, a figure who
behaves in public in ways that Andrea can only imagine in the
privacy of her own innermost fantasies. Ena is also Andrea's dark,
disturbing double, in the sense that she embodies a free, uninhibited
outlook and significantly a cruel, sadistic streak. She thus external-
izes the drives and desires that Andrea represses, but to which she
would like to give vent.

It is therefore annoying and extremely frustrating for the main
protagonist to find that almost the first thing Ena says to her
concerns her uncle Román and the embarrassing reality of Aribau:
'El primer día de curso me había preguntado que si yo era parienta de
un violinista célebre. Recuerdo que la pregunta me pareció absurda y
me hizo reír' (60). In fact, Andrea feels 'casi defraudada' (62) at her
friend's enquiry. She is disappointed and frustrated in several ways.
While she is desperately trying to escape Aribau, her most favoured
friend seems to be demanding access; and having just met Ena, she
has no wish to disappoint her by revealing the truly unflattering
nature of this 'violinista célebre'. She fears the contamination of her
luminous new student world by the fetid, sordid reality of Aribau.
She is ashamed of her connection with her family and would wish to
re-tell its story in a far more romantic light (63). She thus fears Ena's
penetration into her other world, over whose secrets she has
exercised control so far. But, however much she tries to keep these
two worlds separate, she is aware that 'una especie de predestinación
unió a Ena desde el principio a la vida de la calle de Aribau' (68).
Moreover, at the very beginning of her new-found intimacy and
friendship, Andrea feels undermined by her own sense of inferiority
in relation to Ena (in dress, appearance, money, confidence, etc.), so
much so that she flees from the University and from 'la segura
mirada de mi amiga' (63), that unnerving, penetrating gaze which,
like Román's, threatens to invade her innermost secrets.

Though Andrea admires Román, she also feels threatened by
him and resents his power to control and manipulate. This resent-
ment finds expression in Ena. Only Ena can handle Román in his
quest for a soul-mate, only she can equal him in perversity and

cruelty. Ena thus functions in the novel as an instrument of punishment and revenge. Like Gloria before her, she will pay back the dark hero for all the hurt and suffering he has caused the other women characters. Ena may be seen as Laforet's version of the predatory female, the Sadeian woman, who does not suffer but causes suffering. Her principal motive for humbling Román is, of course, to avenge her mother's traumatic experience, but there is more. Recounting a meeting with Román in Part III, which parallels Andrea's close encounter in Part I, Ena asks her friend, '¿Cómo te voy a explicar el juego apasionante en que se convertía aquello para mí?' (267). As with Gloria and her gambling, the gaming metaphor is extended to include human relationships and in particular the game of manipulating masculine identity, which Ena finds tremendously exciting. She describes her contest with Román as 'este duelo entre la frialdad y el dominio de los nervios de Román y mi propia malicia y seguridad...' (267) and prophetically 'Una lucha a muerte' (267). However, even though she taunts and exasperates the old warrior, she is also capable of displaying a certain sophisticated, swooning femininity in the face of the charismatic male, as Andrea finds out when she tries to rescue her friend from her uncle's attempt at seduction and is made to look a complete fool (258).

Ena thus seems to fulfil a series of functions. She acts as Andrea's friend, though none-too-supportive confidante. She takes on the role of saviour or even fairy godmother at several strategic moments, notably through telephone calls or at the end of the novel, when she invites Andrea to Madrid, thus ensuring her unexpected release from Aribau. Ena is also the instrument by which Laforet takes revenge on male oppression, violence and a predatory sexuality; she acts to exorcise the evil force, the poison that inhabits Aribau's degenerate patriarchy and in doing so seems to suggest that female sexuality is deadlier than the male variety. Ena also represents the adolescent female figure of high-bourgeois culture; she embodies bourgeois self-confidence and a powerful ego while Andrea, by contrast, is the terrified petite bourgeoise. And unlike Andrea, who has been taught to believe in the power of literature and is in many ways victimized by her allegiance to the conventions of romantic fiction, Ena breaks the spell. She rebels against literary indoctrination. Indeed, rather than listen to Andrea's version, she enters the story as an actor and creates it for herself first-hand. And by not succumbing to Román, but by provoking his suicide, she leaves the story victorious. Paradoxically and rather annoyingly, however, she also colludes with romantic literature and in the end, by planning to marry Jaime, simply reinforces its power. This is because Ena is not simply a femme fatale. Though real and devastating in their effect on Román, her sadism and cruelty are also a front, we learn, to satisfy family expectations. Ena has another side to her character; she is also a nice girl at heart and it takes her relationship with Andrea to make her realize that this is indeed the case (262). Ena is destined to marry Jaime and this projected event appears to be one of the ways in which Laforet gives an otherwise gloomy, pessimistic novel a happy end. Also, the announcement of marriage signifies Ena's symbolic death as the predatory female. Having given free rein to her 'demonios' or childish desires for a time and having experienced the thrill of entrapping and jilting a much older man, she can now return to normal and settle down.

But is marriage to Jaime a marriage of equals? Ena's love for him is accompanied by the affection she feels towards Andrea. Jaime is divested of the negative features of male relationships and, like Andrea, functions as a companion, a friend and not as a threatening macho figure. In a sense, Ena shares him with Andrea and no one is left out, although the impression is given initially that Ena is simply using Andrea as an excuse in order to see Jaime. None the less, Andrea does not pretend to compete for Jaime's affections and she finds this *ménage à trois* a much happier arrangement than that of monogamy. In the company of her two friends, it seems, the male figure does not represent an obstacle to the relationship between the two women; he is not an authority figure who disrupts female contact. Indeed, Jaime is feminized, he takes on a supportive, protective role, behaves like a mother figure (on their Sunday outings, he lets the girls borrow his raincoat while he happily gets wet, 139) and the two girls behave like sisters. It may be the case, then, that Laforet can only imagine Ena's marriage to a non-threatening, diminished male figure, since traditional male behaviour in the novel normally brings discord to harmonious female relationships.

If we consider Andrea's relationship with Gerardo, we find that it fails calamitously and it does so, it seems, because it is not mediated by another female presence. Gerardo adopts the attitude of the dominant male. Like Román, he intimidates Andrea and makes her feel like a dog (142). His chauvinism is quite apparent: 'no creía en la inteligencia femenina' (143). Also, behind a mask of pity and understanding, he acts like a traditional, authoritarian father figure, offering 'paternales consejos' to Andrea on 'la conveniencia de no andar suelta y loca y de no salir sola con los muchachos' (146). As we have seen, Gerardo briefly gains Andrea's sympathy when he shares her indignation at the defacement of the nude statue of Venus in Montjuich Park and proceeds to clean the red lipstick from 'los labios de mármol hasta que quedaron limpios' (143). The very act of cleansing the statue of the outward signs of sensuality and sinfulness reveals in Gerardo, and more generally in the traditional male psyche, a need to regard woman as pure and totally immune from excessive carnality. His action, which is very much in tune with Angustias's outlook, reinforces the constant preoccupation in the novel to save women from the ever-present temptation of sensuality. He also elicits Andrea's sympathy: 'me sentí súbitamente conmovida' (144), through his soft, confessional tone of voice. Won by this intimacy, Andrea puts her hand on his and then — as if misreading the signals — Gerardo tries to kiss her. As we have already noted, Andrea reacts with a mixture of fear and loathing: 'me subió una oleada de asco por la saliva y el calor de sus labios gordos' (145) and judges him to be no more than a 'semental' (145), acting simply to satisfy his sexual appetite. Andrea as narrator realizes, of course, the naiveté and stupidity of her reaction, yet it shows the extent to which Andrea as actor/agent is still trapped by the traditional conventions of romance (Gerardo is a very poor substitute for the Prince Charming she wants and thinks she deserves). She is still unable to deal with physical or sensual contact and see it as anything other than a threat. In the end, Andrea seems incapable of establishing a

monogamous, heterosexual relationship unless it is mediated by
another female presence or the male figure is somehow feminized
and presents no direct sexual threat.

Andrea is thus an obviously sensual, but extremely inhibited,
young woman. The invitation by the young Pons to attend a ball and
spend the summer with him and his family presents itself as a
possible liberation for Andrea. But she is still very reticent, unable to
cope with the idea of Pons being in love with her, since she imagines
this commits her to him in more intimate and troubling ways: 'Pero
aún estaba detenida por la sensación molesta que el enamoramiento
de Pons me producía. Creía yo que una contestación afirmativa a su
ofrecimiento me ligaba a él por otros lazos que me inquietaban,
porque me parecían falsos' (202). Up to this point, the relationship
with Pons has been one of friendship, in the context of Andrea's
University acquaintances and Pons's artistic friends, the young
'bohemios', in their studio in the *barrio gótico*. Andrea has felt no
anxiety or threat from any of the boys and they, in their turn, have
allowed her into their circle because as Pons points out: 'yo les dije
que tú no te pintabas en absoluto' (153). In other words, unlike Ena,
Andrea represents no threat to them, she is not regarded as a mature,
knowledgeable, sensual woman. However, faced by the prospect of a
one-to-one relationship, with the further possibility that she might
fall in love and thus, in her own eyes, fall into womanhood, only fills
her with dread. She dreams of taking the decisive step into mature,
adult relations, of breaking out of the protective chrysalis (215) and
overcoming her childish fears, but in the end she is simply too afraid
of men. This perhaps explains her view of herself as plain and
ordinary (214) and the fact that she retains a totally infantile view of
beauty and love, longing as she is to become transformed into a
'rubia princesa' (215), just like Ena, her ego-ideal. Andrea is aware,
however, that in order to become a woman, she has to overcome her
typical, spectatorial role (215) and by implication, abandon the
model of behaviour offered by Román, the other compulsive voyeur
of the novel. Rather than the subject, she has to become the object of
the gaze of others, as she surmises: 'Tal vez el sentido de la vida para
una mujer consiste únicamente en ser descubierta así, mirada de

manera que ella se sienta irradiante de luz. No en mirar [...]' (215).
Unfortunately, her great opportunity to occupy centre stage and
make the decisive break is a total failure.

The ball at Pons's house is a disaster, for which Andrea largely
blames poor Pons. On being introduced to Pons's mother, Andrea is
immediately struck by the woman's eyes, 'la mirada suya,
indefinible, dirigida a mis viejos zapatos' (218); she interprets this
gaze as one of disapproval and rejection. She then feels 'angustiada
por la pobreza de mi atavío' (218). Her sense of inferiority wells up
as she contemplates the other guests: 'Predominaban las muchachas
bonitas [...] Me sentía muy tímida entre ellas' (218). Andrea's shame
and guilt at her appearance turn into despair: 'Casi tenía ganas de
llorar [...]' (218), 'me sentí un poco ridícula' (219). The ball thus
becomes an ironic reversal of the Cinderella story, in which the glass
slippers are transformed into Andrea's old shoes. Pons is then made
to shoulder the responsibility, as Andrea projects onto him her inner
fears: 'Mi amigo [...] sin duda, se sentía avergonzado de mí' (221).
The point is, however, that Andrea herself is mainly to blame for her
own misfortune. She makes little or no effort to become involved at
the dance and to mix with the guests; she refuses to dance with Pons
and is unable to make him interested in her. She obviously wants the
boy's attention, in order to confirm that she is attractive; but while
she demands Pons's affection, she seems incapable of giving it
herself. It is as if she had inherited Román's childish need for
someone to feed her own narcissism. And of course, had she wished,
she could have bought some new shoes, just as she bought presents
and a new blouse for the elegant soirée at Ena's house. So Andrea
can make an effort when she wants to. We might infer, therefore,
that Andrea was far more interested in her relationship with Ena than
in a possible love affair with Pons. In the end, Andrea intuits her
own responsibility in the matter: 'Quizá lo había estropeado todo la
mirada primera que dirigió su madre a mis zapatos... O quizá era
culpa mía' (221). The example of Pons's ball seems to confirm the
impression that Andrea is still scared and inhibited and is unable to
break out of her passive, spectatorial role: 'Imposible salirme de él.
Imposible libertarme' (224). To what extent, we may ask, does the

main protagonist develop into a mature young woman? How far is Laforet's novel a story of female development? This is the subject of the following chapter.

4. A Novel of Female Development?

Nada has been viewed predominantly as a female version of a *Bildungsroman*, that is, a novel which concentrates on the development of one main character from youth to some form of adulthood. Michael Thomas, for example, argues that the novel shows 'a gradual progression in Andrea towards mature action and thought' and that the protagonist is finally 'transformed from an unrealistic dreamer, an unassertive, unforgiving, self-centred child into a hopeful, compassionate, decisive adult' (*27*, pp.58, 72). Marsha Collins is another critic who regards *Nada* as having to do with 'the agonized maturation of the young', 'the challenge of forging one's being in the modern world', 'the gradual acquisition of self-hood' (*8*, p.298). From a feminist perspective, Sara Schyfter emphasizes the theme of female friendship in the novel and sees Andrea achieving 'un sentido claro de dirección y autosuficiencia, un estado mental que ha alcanzado por sí sola y no a través de la relación con un hombre' (*24*, p.90). In short, *Nada* is widely regarded as a novel of education, charting the difficult passage from childhood innocence to adult understanding, dependence to independence, ignorance to knowledge. Critics such as Villegas (*30*, pp.178-79) also seem to accept that, in reaching adulthood, the main protagonist develops into a full, coherent, human subject and acquires a secure, stable identity. Interestingly, the critics tend not to elaborate on their notions of adulthood, maturity, self-hood, whose meanings are never made very clear and in some cases are simply taken for granted. Nor do they acknowledge that, at least since Freud and Lacan, our ideas concerning identity and subjectivity have been radically unsettled.[3]

---

[3] For a useful and fairly accessible introduction to Freud and Lacan, see Terry Eagleton, *Literary Theory* (Oxford: Basil Blackwell, 1983), especially pp.161-71.

The notion of a stable, fully-formed, human subject emerging from a gradual process of development has always been problematic and has become increasingly so in the modern era.

Leaving aside these more theoretical considerations, it can still be argued that Laforet's novel presents certain signs or threads of character development. Firstly, development is implied in its chronological order. *Nada* deals with a decisive year in the life of the main protagonist (from October to the following September), a period of time which has a clear beginning and end and arguably functions as a discrete, separable stage, after which she enters an apparently new phase in her life. Secondly, a change is obviously suggested by Andrea's move to Madrid at the end of the novel. She seems to fulfil her ambitions of renewing personal friendships and achieving social and class mobility, moving to the capital to work, study, and at some stage find a place of her own. Thirdly, development seems to be built into *Nada's* narrative structure, which we might loosely describe as an 'enclosure-escape' story. The novel begins and ends with a journey, one which precedes Andrea's entry into the city of Barcelona and another which marks her exit from it. Entry and exit are made at different times (midnight as against early morning) by different means of transport (train as against chauffeur-driven limousine) and give rise to different connotations (darkness is contrasted with light, the gloomy mansion of Aribau is symbolically exorcised by the morning sunlight, the hellish city of Barcelona is finally left behind). For the main protagonist, therefore, entrapment is apparently followed by what she herself terms 'una liberación' (294). She is figuratively released from captivity and given another chance for freedom. And in contrast to the two traditional routes for women proposed in the novel, marriage or the convent, which are taken up by the *abuela,* Gloria, Angustias, Margarita and Ena, Andrea's escape reveals a third route, based on female friendship. Thus, for the protagonist, a whole series of negative elements and associations are succeeded by their opposite. A major qualitative change seems to take place.

Fourthly, and perhaps most importantly, development is indicated through the act of writing. The latter is indecisively located. We are not told when or from where Andrea composes her story; we are not told why she is writing; nor are we given any indication of the amount of time elapsed between the end of her experiences, on which the narrative is based, and their reconstruction and re-elaboration in writing. The gap between leaving Aribau and becoming established in Madrid — a gap which is never filled — constitutes the main marker of development in the story: the doubleness of the narrating I, the split between protagonist and narrator, between immature experience and mature utterance. This split, which takes the form of a shifting and mobile relationship between Andrea as actor and narrator, is indicated by various means: verbs of recall (e.g. 'recuerdo que', 12; 'creo que pensé', 27); shifts of tense, from preterite into perfect (e.g. 'he hecho tantos juicios equivocados...', 27; 'La música de Román, que nunca más he vuelto a oír', 41); the widespread use of parentheses, which enclose intimate asides made to the reader and suggest a need to share secrets on the part of the narrator (e.g. pp.25, 26, 106, 157, 230); reflections and judgements which only the narrator could make (e.g. 'En realidad, mi pena de chiquilla desilusionada no merecía tanto aparato', 224; 'Encontraba idiota sentir otra vez aquella ansiosa expectación [...]', 294). So, long before we can guess how the narrator has changed, her voice alerts us that she has. Moreover, she does appear to have developed a more cautious and compassionate understanding of the different characters, e.g. towards Angustias and especially towards Román (286). Andrea also seems better able to distinguish between reality and appearances and has apparently overcome her naive belief in the mythology of romantic love. However, a complicating factor is that, like that of Andrea-protagonist, the narrator's stance is frequently one of uncertainty and indecision; a number of her statements about the past are qualified by 'quizá'. She also regards some of her judgements as possibly erroneous, even up to the time of writing, as happens, for example, when she reflects on her attitude towards Angustias: 'Y la juzgaba, sin ninguna compasión, corta de luces y autoritaria. He hecho tantos juicios equivocados en mi vida, que aún no sé si éste era verdadero' (27).

A further marker of development, already alluded to, is the fact that the narrator apparently writes from a position of plenitude and fulfilment. She has managed to escape the nightmarish world of Aribau and move up into the luminous, prosperous and stable world of Ena's family. She thus realizes the dream with which she entered the novel, though she does so, not through her own step-family, but through another. She thus symbolically overcomes her condition of orphanhood by being adopted by a surrogate family, a move which suggests that those nearest (i.e. Aribau) are not always dearest. Andrea's entry into a higher social class and her rise to womanhood are also accompanied by the reduction and finally the self-elimination of one of the figures whose influence she had to reject in order to gain independence, i.e. Román. To all intents and purposes, then, the protagonist's ambitions and desires seem to be amply fulfilled. A new life beckons, in the company of her closest friends. We thus have what appears to be a happy ending, a cosy romance come true. Andrea has not yet found a mate for herself, but with the example of Ena and Jaime before her (they plan to marry once Jaime finishes his degree) and her new understanding of the pitfalls of love and romance, she is in a better position to make the right choice, if it presents itself.

All the signs discussed above seem to point towards Andrea's progressive maturation. There is something slightly puzzling and paradoxical, however, about this novelistic resolution. Andrea's great expectations look as if they will be fulfilled, but if this happens, it does so offstage. The novel does not concern itself with the story of Andrea's success, which is left unnarrated. In fact, it does the precise opposite. *Nada* is the story of the non-fulfilment of Andrea's dreams, it is a cautionary tale of how not to behave and how not to trust in childish notions of romance. Moreover, Andrea's escape from Aribau and her independence are achieved through absolutely no effort on her part. Her salvation is the product of a *deus ex machina,* an external agent, a providential, fairy-godmother figure played by Ena and her letter of invitation to Madrid. (This repeats the situation at the beginning of the novel when cousin Isabel wrote to Aribau in order to ask Angustias to take charge of Andrea. Then, however,

Andrea had actively engineered her own expulsion from the village (39); now, a year later, things are different; indeed, Andrea is almost resigned to staying at Aribau). In other words, the protagonist's liberation and personal fulfilment are not earned through struggle, but bestowed upon her from above. This feature clearly complicates the way the novel has been conventionally classified as a *Bildungsroman*. Moreover, is Andrea writing from a position of plenitude and fulfilment? Is everything going smoothly? Is she happy? Has she really developed into a mature, self-confident, compassionate adult, as the dominant interpretative framework suggests?

These questions arise because rather than conforming to the widely-accepted literary model of male *Bildung* (purposeful, linear development, overcoming obstacles through individual effort and struggle) or modern versions of female *Bildung* (involving the protagonist in a conscious, willed separation from male-defined norms), *Nada* presents almost the opposite picture. The problem is that the main protagonist seems excessively passive as a character. On occasion she will do things in response to another's invitation or entreaty, such as her meeting with Román in his room, her outing with Gerardo, her descent into the *barrio gótico* in pursuit of Juan, her attendance at Pons's ball, her effort to save Ena from Román. But, on the whole, she does not act in the conventional sense of initiating things, of planning and executing ideas, of carrying them through, of actively engaging in her quest for independence through some conscious resolve or driving ambition. On the contrary, perhaps in the manner of many nineteenth-century literary heroines (predominantly silent, brooding, coy, blushing), Andrea is the object, rarely the subject of actions or events. Things happen to her and are done for her. In fact, she finds it extraordinarily difficult to act or be active (e.g. presented with the opportunity of reassuring an enraged Juan about Gloria's fidelity, 'No hice nada' (175); also, during her attempt to save Ena, it is only after considerable hesitation (256) that she knocks on Román's door). On the whole, she feels much safer looking on, observing the actions of others, adopting a withdrawn, voyeuristic role. Also, her feelings, desires and sensuality are expressed through fevers, dreams, hallucinations and neuroses and lived out in other characters. It is as if Andrea projects onto others those inner drives and intensities of feeling she cannot allow herself to release. She is perfectly aware of her spectatorial position: 'Yo tenía un pequeño y ruin papel de espectadora. Imposible salirme de él. Imposible libertarme' (224). But, as occurred at Pons's ball, it is as if Andrea does not really want to escape and transcend her childish voyeurism. It is a condition which, though responding to the burden of sexual repression, actually fulfils her own perceived inadequacies and lacks and through which she can derive pleasure and excitement (at a distance) with minimal personal risk.

Notwithstanding the above comments, most critics continue to support the idea of Andrea's personal maturation and development. And they do so by invoking the conventional 'hurdles/obstacles' model of male development, involving a series of difficulties or challenges which the protagonist has to negotiate. They tend to cite, for example, the 'ambiente opresivo' (57) of Aribau, its role as a 'prisión correccional' (64), from which Andrea has to escape. However, they tend to ignore the fact that, for the protagonist, Aribau 'había llegado a constituir el único interés de mi vida' (43). Lacking other outlets, Andrea becomes fascinated, even obsessed by Aribau, its eccentric inhabitants and their bizarre, and as yet secret, biographies. In similar fashion, critical opinion usually refers to Andrea's struggle to separate herself from her oppressive and authoritarian aunt Angustias: 'Me di cuenta de que podía soportarlo todo [...] Todo menos su autoridad sobre mí. Era aquello lo que me había ahogado al llegar a Barcelona [...] lo que mataba mis iniciativas: aquella mirada de Angustias' (99). Andrea feels oppressed by her aunt's powerful, penetrating gaze, a gaze of reproach and repression, which induces feelings of guilt and anxiety. Yet, at the same time, Angustias 'era un ser recto y bueno a su manera entre aquellos locos. Un ser más completo y vigoroso que los demás...' (99). In other words, the very obstacles to Andrea's development are regarded ambivalently by her; the house is oppressive but no less fascinating; Angustias may be authoritarian, but she is also fair and honest in her own way and physically attractive to

Andrea. Here, we again encounter the romantic dualism which pervades the novel, the way the characters are internally divided and the way they repel but also attract. Obstacles become incitements to the protagonist's interest and imagination. The hurdles which she is supposed to overcome are the very things which give meaning to her life. Does she resolve any of these difficulties through her own initiative? In the face of Angustias's repressions, Andrea admits that 'Yo no concebía entonces más resistencia que la pasiva' (32). And with her aunt's departure for the convent, Andrea achieves freedom without so much as a cross word: 'en aquel momento parecía que había llegado la hora de conseguirlo sin el menor trabajo por mi parte' (108). In the case of Román, Andrea does manage to overcome her initial illusions, see his evil side and free herself from his malign influence. But it is only through Ena's intervention and not through her own action or initiative that this happens. Moreover, Román commits suicide, thus relieving Andrea of the burden of freeing herself. And significantly, at the end of Part III, after the suicide, Andrea goes up to his room and feels 'Una atroz añoranza de sus manos sobre el violín' (286), that is, a desire to repeat and recapture previously pleasurable moments. So, rather than emerging as fully-emancipated and independent, Andrea somehow still appears to be in thrall to the dark hero, expressing a profound nostalgia for his presence. As the grandmother points out, things are not always what they seem. On the surface, Andrea appears to follow a gradual path of development from immaturity to maturity, along which she overcomes certain obstacles. However, below that surface, she changes very little and does almost nothing to achieve her goals; this suggests that she is not really developing at all and that the 'obstacles' model of male *Bildung* might well be inappropriate. We are thus faced with a paradox. *Nada* seems to contain two contradictory movements or pulls, one forwards (suggesting development) but also another which is directed backwards (suggesting a form of regression to a pre-adolescent or childhood phase).

As previously noted, the narrator tells us nothing of what has happened since she left Aribau. She refuses to tell us where she is, how she is, whether she is still on friendly terms with Ena and whether her new-found freedom has fulfilled her expectations or not. The main thrust of the narrative therefore is backwards, responding to a desire to relive and re-elaborate the past. On the surface, Andrea is presumably cured of the romantic nonsense with which she entered Aribau. But, the break with childhood fantasies and illusions is far from clear. Indeed, the text of *Nada* may be seen as an exercise in nostalgia. Far from expressing a desire to break with the past, the story is arguably an imaginative attempt to hold onto it, to embrace and preserve it, as if the experience of Aribau now constituted a crucial *lack* for the protagonist, which she wished to recover and relive. So, if Andrea is the silent heroine during her stay at Aribau, she breaks her silence in writing. Writing, story-telling, narrativizing experience are activities which she finds immensely pleasurable and necessary. They constitute her active, interventionist side and through them she is able to recapture those moments of excitement and pleasure which, in the here and now, are presumably missing. Laforet's novel may be the story of a young girl's sentimental education and gradual acquisition of adult judgement and knowledge. Yet, at the same time, the novel speaks of a powerful desire to return, to recapture and inhabit the past of childhood memories.

So alongside the view of *Nada* as *Bildungsroman*, we find its other, a plot of inner development, which rather than going forwards moves backwards. It searches out origins and retraces the drama of a maturation that is highly ambiguous, since Andrea is seemingly poised between self-sufficiency (Madrid) and her desire to re-experience Aribau. What seems to dominate in *Nada* is a structure of repetitions rather than progressions, a pattern of returns and reenactments of scenes already performed by the other characters and surveyed by the protagonist. As narrator, Andrea watches herself as actor watching these re-presentations. The novel is thus characterized by its circularity. For example, at the end of the novel, though the protagonist is less full of her girlish illusions, her final attitude recalls her naive optimism at the beginning of the novel: 'No tenía ahora las mismas ilusiones, pero aquella partida me emocionaba como una liberación' (294). This is exactly how she regarded her move from the village to the city of Barcelona. A pattern thus begins to emerge whereby Andrea moves from one form of enclosure to another, thinking each time that the move will be a liberation, but in reality, it turns out to be the opposite. Each time, the place of reception (the village, Barcelona, and now Madrid) is fantasized as a solution to Andrea's desires and each time the dream becomes a nightmare, illusion is followed by disillusionment in a repeating cycle. (We are not told how things are in Madrid; this silence may indicate that Andrea is not altogether happy. The fact that she decides to write of her experiences at Aribau and re-enter the past may also suggest that Ena is unavailable as the confidante for the oral version of the story. The drive to write may thus respond to dissatisfaction as much as to a new-found security in Madrid.) So alongside the view of *Nada* as a novel of female development, it is readable as a novel of stasis, circularity, repetition and entrapment, in which Andrea is fated to experience and repeat the same.

One feature which might support this alternative view is that, at the end of the novel, the split between Andrea as actor and narrator is not closed; there is no merging of these functions and no presentation of events from a unified viewpoint. At the end of the novel, there is no sense of narrative closure, no reaching a point of completion; the reader does not know all there is to know. Indeed, the narrator knows far more than she is willing to reveal and the enigma lingers on beyond the apparently happy end. So, there is little sense of a full, confident subject, willing to disclose details, external and internal to the text. Indeed, as Laforet herself points out 'puse el relato en boca de una jovencilla que es casi una sombra que cuenta'.[4] The author's own view of her narrator as 'una sombra', a shadowy, ghostly figure, seems to add weight to the argument that Andrea does not really develop into a strong, decisive, self-confident adult. And, as we have seen, even as an actor in the story, Andrea mainly functions in a subordinate, shadowy, voyeuristic role. In fact, it is extremely difficult to conceive of Andrea as a solid subject, gradually moving forwards and developing a sense of selfhood. For if we begin to interrogate Andrea's notion of self, it becomes clear that it is defined by and lived through others. One of the overriding

---

[4] *Mis páginas mejores*, p.13.

features of Andrea's behaviour in the novel is that she searches, not
for herself, but for everything that is not herself. She gravitates
towards images of difference, images that contrast with her own self-
image as a boring, 'plain Jane' figure. She is thus instantly attracted
to Román's physical beauty and eccentric behaviour, to Ena's beauty,
cunning and cruelty, to Angustias's sense of order, to the grandmother's ability to be compassionate and indulgent. In short, Andrea
defines herself through others or rather, through her own limited,
fantasized perceptions of others. Andrea says of Ena: 'Me hizo sentirme todo lo que no era: rica y feliz' (70). Ena thus embodies all the
qualities Andrea would like to have but could never achieve. And
even when Andrea is the victim of Ena's sarcasm and cruelty, she is
still prepared to ignore her friend's negative side and by implication
indulge in a conscious form of self-deception. Similarly, Andrea is
aware that Ena is using her as an excuse in order to cover for her
outings with Jaime; yet she regards her inclusion in these trips as
'una dicha concedida a pocos seres humanos' and feels 'arrastrada en
ese halo casi palpable que irradia una pareja de enamorados y que
hace que el mundo vibre más [...] y sea más infinito y más profundo'
(139). Andrea achieves identity, then, by fantasizing her outings with
Ena and Jaime as privileged moments and by seeing her friends as
protector figures, people in whom she can find understanding,
compassion, warmth and an idealized version of what she would like
herself to be. Andrea thus seems to be in search, not of herself as a
separate entity, but of characters who act as her own imagined,
multiple selves and in whom she can simply merge and dissolve.

On the whole, then, Andrea is not an agent for narrative
change. Her dominant position is that of passivity, her mode of
resistance, as we have seen, is to resign herself. And apart from her
fascination with classical art and the grandeur of a more settled,
bourgeois past, her overriding passion is to be left alone to do her
own thing: 'el único deseo de mi vida ha sido que me dejen en paz
para hacer mi capricho' (108). Yet she does little or nothing to
achieve this. Most of her actions are reactions to the actions of
others. Only near the end of the novel does she express the thrill of
being active when she is about to intervene between Ena and Román

(255). Unfortunately, her 'misión providencial' (254), as she calls it, rebounds on her and is met with Ena's biting sarcasm: 'Andrea ¿por qué eres tan trágica, querida?', 259). In Andrea's case, action seems positively counterproductive and her fear of failure, of looking foolish, may partly explain her reluctance to act. With a lack of drive in Andrea, we thus have psychological and to some extent narrative paralysis. Andrea's growth as a character is almost imperceptible. Like a child, she learns through listening, overhearing, spying. And given the fact that, as a character, she is almost lacking in personality traits (only slowly and randomly does the odd indication emerge), she comes over as a rather formless sensibility, which only takes on a rudimentary shape in heated situations and through reactions to the initiatives of others. As previously noted, Andrea has to be pushed into action; her formation as a character thus emerges through her trying to resist others' urge to shape her, Angustias being the obvious case in point. In short, other characters are the motivations for Andrea's self-discovery. Narrative and character development thus seem to operate through a process of inter-personal friction which leaves traces on Andrea. Also, given the way the rhythm of the novel depends on the shifting relations between order and disorder, law and passion, learning becomes a process of recognition that the characters are split into idealized and demonized versions. The main protagonist and the other characters all indulge in a series of misrecognitions, fantasies and wish-fulfilments, projecting themselves into other characters. They thus strain to assert their ideal versions over more mundane ones. This echoes and reaffirms that basic yearning in Andrea for beauty and sensitivity while finding ugliness and despotism at Aribau. Overall, characters and character development seem to emerge in response to desire, to a desire to find in others their own lack, no matter how blatant the gap between created image and actual behaviour. Also, the characters — with Andrea as perhaps the main culprit — are prepared to tolerate the dark and threatening side of others and exonerate their cruelty through wilful repression of the evidence (the grandmother consistently defends her two sons, despite their manic behaviour;

Andrea always defends Ena, even though she recognizes her cruelty
and knows she is being used by her).

In short, other characters in the novel function as parts or
versions of Andrea. They operate as a series of negations of her
desires (Angustias tries to stamp out her rebelliousness; Román's
anarchic, threatening male sexuality and Ena's sadistic activities
negate her desire for beauty and stability). But they also act as
affirmations of her deepest fantasies (Román represents maturity and
an access to sexual knowledge; Ena operates as Andrea's ego-ideal;
Gloria stands for the sensuous woman). It is as if Andrea as
writer/narrator has re-imagined these characters in an extreme form,
a form which she finds thrilling and attractive, and then decides to
withdraw. They act in, on and for her, replacing her activity by
theirs. They assume her demands for control and at the same time
fulfil her deepest, uncontrolled desires. The novel thus seems to steer
a passage between images of attraction and beauty (which promise
the thrill of disruption) and images of law and control (which satisfy
the demand for stability). Moving through the novel, presented with
all these images, Andrea does not emerge as a fully-formed
character. Rather, she is an absence which is given shape through
others, others who are no more than externalizations of her own
emotions; she simply reacts to these personifications of her desires.
She thus seems to move among her own avatars (swinging between
attraction and repulsion, fascination and deception), reacting to
characters who offer her versions of herself which she continually
disowns and desires at the same time. This produces an I, a self,
which is remote, distant from its own faculties, an entity beside and
beyond itself, separate from the things of which it is composed. As a
subject, then, Andrea is not stable and fully-formed, but highly
fragmented; she is everywhere and nowhere; the inside of the self
stands on the outside, different bits of her are embodied and personi-
fied in other characters. (As we have seen, the requirement for
obedience, control and repression calls up Angustias; the demand for
passion and sensuality summons Román or Gloria; the Sadeian
woman means Ena; the ideal couple, destined for harmonious
matrimony, brings up Ena and Jaime; and as the last example shows,

all of these characters play more than one role, their dominant features are reversible, subject to inversion and change.) Andrea thus moves through a world that moves through her. The notion of the substantive, stable subject and her development into a mature, independent self thus appear illusory. Indeed, that final, fully-developed adult remains immaterial, dispersed as it is into its many secondary incarnations, through Andrea's own projections onto others and through others' fantasized images of her. It would seem therefore that there is a problem in locating the self which speaks to the reader, a self which combines an intimate mode of address to the reader with manifest evasions and which, at the same time, dissolves and disperses into others. If this is so, then can we continue to regard *Nada* as a *Bildungsroman*? Is there still a self which we can say has developed?

The dominant critical view argues that Andrea's sensibility changes and matures, that her personality coheres, if only as a result of the shift from enclosure to apparent freedom in Madrid. But what has changed? She may not have the same illusions as before yet she still regards her exit from Barcelona with the same childish optimism she experienced at the beginning of the novel (294). Moreover, there is no necessary link between exposure to different characters and the development of an integrated self. Andrea's greater compassion and understanding of Román or Ena may not make her a wiser person. On the contrary, given the behaviour of these characters, such an attitude recalls the misplaced indulgence heaped on Juan and Román by the grandmother. In the end, by writing, Andrea repeats earlier compulsions and shows she has learnt very little. What changes in the novel happens around her. *Nada* is full of personal catastrophe (wife-beating, madness, sadism, maso-chism, suicide, etc.); none of these befalls the protagonist, though they do stimulate her imagination. Development, in Andrea's case, turns out to be that of those around her; her own growth is problematic and unclear and it may well be a visual illusion. More-over, the activities of other characters (which represent extreme forms of desire) save the protagonist from the perils of extremism; her potential excesses are thus tempered by the excesses of others. If this is *Bildung* or development, then it is *Bildung* by negative example. Andrea learns how not to be, she learns what she must avoid, i.e. excess in all its forms (passion, sensuality, sadism, etc). Yet, through writing, she can re-experience all of these vicariously without having to deal with the consequences.

5. *Style and Imagery*

Nada has usually been regarded as a fairly derivative, bookish version of a family romance, overly indebted to other literary models and genres, of which, it is said, it is little more than a re-write. As a result, its languages and stylistic resources have been taken as very much a distillation and re-working of those of other narrative discourses. It may seem paradoxical, therefore, that part of the novel's initial critical success had to do with the novelty of its style. An unnamed reviewer in *Mundo* in 1945 saw the novel as 'llena de juventud, de fuerza, de originalidad espontánea'; it was a 'drama sombrío, violento, impresionante' in which 'alterna la nota de ternura, casi infantil, con las pinceladas de brutalidad y tristeza'.[5] As this and other critics pointed out, *Nada* was noteworthy for its freshness, vitality, directness, spontaneity and punch. Indeed, some critics were so surprised by the novel's truculence and lurid picture of family crisis and psychological break-down that they thought it had been written by a man or at the very least, by a much older woman.[6] Part of the reason for these reactions and confusions has to do with the novel's style and with the way Andrea, as actor, relates to her novelistic world. This relationship is neatly encapsulated in the poetic fragment taken from Juan Ramón Jiménez, which precedes the text of the novel, and stresses the importance of sensory perception and awareness as a basis for understanding the world. In other words, reality and truth are functions, not so much of the cognitive processes or reflexive thought, but of the immediate and un-mediated response of the senses to external stimuli. Andrea is not a

---

[5] *Mundo* (15 July 1945).
[6] Manuel Fernández Almagro, *ABC* (13 Aug. 1945); Juan Eduardo Zúñiga, *La Estafeta Literaria* (10 July 1945); Manuel Linares, *Razón y Fe* (September 1946).

character who thinks a great deal or who relies on logic and reason to read the world. Rather, she responds intuitively to events, relies on her feelings to guide her and arguably over-interprets reality. The narrator in the novel tries to reproduce this impulsive, irrational, child-like relationship to the world by emphasizing Andrea's innocence, naivety, confusion and inability to draw conclusions. By identifying with the character of Andrea, the reader is put into a similar relationship to her crisis-ridden yet momentarily luminous world and this may account, in part, for the novel's directness and immediacy of impact. Of course, in more specific terms, such features are also effects of linguistic choices and depend on the author's selection and exploitation of stylistic resources, aspects of which we shall consider below.

As previously noted, *Nada* is not difficult or demanding reading. Its language is unashamedly conventional and common-place and draws on a range of clearly recognizable stylistic devices, an obvious one being personification. With considerable frequency, but mainly at moments of excitement or tension, Andrea endows inanimate objects with human or animal qualities. For example, at the beginning of the novel and reinforcing the protagonist's 'sensación confusa' (12) of the city, the street lamps are viewed as 'centinelas borrachos de soledad' (12); in the bathroom at Aribau, the peeling walls remind the protagonist of toothless mouths: 'los desconchados abrían sus bocas desdentadas rezumantes de humedad' (17); in the *barrio gótico*, 'Los anuncios guiñaban sus ojos en un juego pesado' (172); the city streets at night, 'oscuras y fétidas', exude 'un vaho rojizo' (176); after Pons's ball, the shopwindows resemble 'una hilera de ojos amarillos o blancos que mirasen desde sus oscuras cuencas' (225); as Andrea climbs the stairs to Román's flat on her mission to save Ena, 'la escalera me cogió entre sus garras' (255), etc. Of course, as we have seen, personification has its counterpart in the novel in the widespread use of animal imagery. In this regard, comparisons are usually based on very familiar, usually domestic, creatures, the most commonplace being cats, dogs and birds, though occasionally the snake and the pig make an appearance. Also, animal images are suggestive not only of character traits and behaviour, as discussed in chapter 3, but they are also used to describe and vivify inanimate objects, such as the flat at Aribau: ' La casa se quedó llena de ecos, gruñendo como un animal viejo' (98); on St Johns Eve, in her room, Andrea stands 'con las orejas tendidas a los susurros de la casa' (202); in one of Aribau's main rooms, Andrea is steeped in the strangely pulsating shadows cast by the furniture 'que la luz de la vela hinchaba llenando de palpitaciones y profunda vida' (18). These simple, perhaps clichéd, comparisons are none the less quite effective in evoking strange, uncanny atmospheres and in reminding the reader of Andrea's sensory relation to the world.

Also, such references are by no means random, but correspond to a larger network of related and repeated image clusters, which are sustained throughout the novel and clearly foreground the narrator's presence. To take just one intriguing example, there is the case of Román's suicide, which is unexpected as well as unexplained, but which is gradually built up through foreshadowing and intra-textual reference. The latter is based on a series of metaphors related to the slaughter of animals, particularly the pig. Román is clearly an aggressive, unstable character whose infantile rage is channelled into two different though related drives: one is a clear desire to hurt other people and the other is a wish for self-annihilation. Almost as soon as we meet him, we find him indulging in his oft-repeated threat to kill Juan: 'Te debiera haber matado hace mucho tiempo' (29). He also projects his aggression onto his dog Trueno and, making one of several significant references to the slaughter of pigs, threatens to slit its throat: 'Este Trueno [...] se está volviendo demasiado decadente [...] Amigo mío, si sigues así te degollaré como a un cerdo' (182). Here we see Román apparently announcing the manner of his own death, a death which is clearly prefigured by Andrea's observation on her first visit to his garret, early in the novel: 'Luego, se tumbaba en la cama [...] como si se hubiera echado para morir fumando' (40). Later, after his attempts to resurrect his affair with Gloria are dashed and she rejects him, her words are again chillingly prophetic: 'No sería por ti, si yo lloraba. Te quiero igual que al cerdo que se lleva al matadero' (205). Gloria's reference clearly parallels and repeats

Román's earlier threat to murder his own dog. Soon after, Román bites Trueno and draws blood (210). Ena refers to Román's 'espíritu de pocilga' (264). And sure enough, having been rejected once again by a woman, this time by Ena, he turns his aggression onto himself. Antonia finds him 'tirado en el suelo, ensangrentado como una bestia' (276), a victim of his own suicidal rage. The animal imagery, the linkage between the beast (the pig) and ritual slaughter, are thus sustained and carried even beyond Román's suicide, since his ghost appears to Juan, inciting him to slit Gloria's throat: 'Dice que soy un cerdo [...] Un día me enseñó una navaja grande que [...] llevaba por si tardaba media hora más para cortarme el cuello [...] Dice que Román se le aparece todas las noches para aconsejarle que me mate...' (290). It is obviously the narrator who is responsible for these examples of intra-textual reference. She is already aware of the outcome of events well before the reader and in some cases perhaps overplays her hand and makes her foreshadowing too obvious. Even so, the repetition and inter-linking of these references do act as an aid to narrative cohesion. Interestingly, it seems that Andrea's experience of pigs relates to her stay at her cousin Isabel's, a reference which is prompted by the eyes of Jerónimo Sanz: 'Sus ojos oscuros, casi sin blanco, me recordaban a los de los cerdos que criaba Isabel en el pueblo' (81).

The animal imagery in *Nada* is accompanied by the extensive and detailed use of water imagery, as Thompson has shown (*28*). Indeed, references to water, waves, rain, showers, storms, rivers, currents, boats, ships and the sea abound in the novel. To take just a few references from the early part of *Nada* we find: Andrea regards herself as 'una gota entre la corriente' (11) on arriving at the Estación de Francia; the coach which takes her to Aribau produces 'una estela de ruido' (13); the air in Aribau is 'estancado y podrido' (15); the lugubrious atmosphere of Aribau and the appearance of its bizarre inhabitants make Andrea feel estranged and filthy, from which she finds fleeting relief in a cold, refreshing, protective shower: '¡Qué alivio el agua helada sobre mi cuerpo!' (17), 'Bruscamente cerré la ducha, el cristalino y protector hechizo, y quedé sola entre la suciedad de las cosas' (18); Gloria's chatter reminds her of the rain:

'Su charla insubstantial me parecía el rumor de la lluvia [...]' (37); Román's room is a 'remanso' (40), where Andrea imbibes his music 'como una lluvia la tierra áspera' (41); Román likens Aribau to 'un barco que se hunde' (40); its inhabitants are 'las pobres ratas que, al ver el agua, no sabemos qué hacer' (40).

Thompson has applied the novel's water imagery to a more general argument concerning the development of the main protagonist. He borrows from another critic, Wilma Newberry (*21*), the linkage between fire and water and midsummer customs. He then relates this feature to the fact that Laforet uses the 'víspera de San Juan' (a night of 'brujerías' and 'milagros' (202), as Andrea informs us) as a means of reversing and subverting the main protagonist's romantic expectations. Thompson's basic idea is that Andrea's negative experience of St John's Eve, traditionally seen as propitious for love and romance, constitutes a symbolic baptism, a mortification from which Andrea emerges anew, cleansed and refreshed, with new and greater powers of perception and action. Thus, after the disaster of Pons's ball, Andrea is supposedly cleansed of her childish illusions and is now better able to act and to prevent herself from being swept along, as usual, by the flow of events (255). In other words, water fulfils the dual function of purification and regeneration. Also, at the symbolic level, Thompson sees the water imagery as a figurative means of indicating Andrea's progressive personal development and of reasserting the view of *Nada* as a *Bildungsroman*. The idea that through water Andrea gradually washes away the old self (the self which is still in thrall to fairy tales and childrens' stories) to uncover a new, self-confident adult, emancipated from her girlish illusions, is an ingenious and intriguing one. Thompson is clearly correct to view the water imagery, in part, as a mode of symbolic cleansing and purgation, as when Andrea takes a shower after Román's death and tries to wash away the guilt she feels (278). But whether the water imagery relates, in broader terms, to Andrea's development into a mature, independent adult is a debatable point.

As noted in chapter 4, Andrea's character development in the novel is ambiguous and problematic. Moreover, if it takes place at all, it does so outside the space of the written narrative. During her year at Aribau, all the indications suggest that she fails to transcend her girlish outlook. Significantly, Román refers to Andrea's immaturity in the following terms: 'Tú eres una criatura... "lo bueno", "lo malo", "lo que me gusta", "lo que me da la gana de hacer"...todo eso es lo que tú tienes metido en la cabeza con una claridad de niño' (90). This parallels almost exactly the very childish way in which Andrea defines her own wishes in life: 'pues el único deseo de mi vida ha sido que me dejen en paz hacer mi capricho' (108). Andrea, it would seem, is still the little child at heart, the 'criatura'. If the process of personal maturation is unclear, then the idea that the water imagery illustrates the process also begins to look doubtful.

I should like to approach the novel's water imagery from a slightly different angle and propose that rather than expressing a new awareness in the protagonist, through a form of symbolic baptism, it functions as a refuge from the vicissitudes of life and arguably reinforces Andrea's infantile tendencies. For example, when musing on whether to accept Pons's invitation to spend the summer with him on the coast, she refers to the beaches and the sea as means of escape from Aribau: 'Sentí al mismo tiempo [...] como un anhelo y un deseo rabioso de despreocupación. De poder libertarme. De aceptar su invitación y poder tumbarme en las playas que él me ofrecía sintiendo pasar las horas como en un cuento de niños, fugada de aquel mundo abrumador que me rodeaba' (202). Also, referring to the previous summer spent at her cousin's house in the country and to the nearby river, Andrea remarks on the pleasure she found in swimming and hints at the satisfying and almost erotic experience of floating in the shadowy water: 'El río aquel [...] doblándose en deliciosos recodos [...] En verano se llenaba de sombras verdes que temblaban entre mis brazos al nadar [...] Si me dejaba arrastrar por la corriente, aquellas sombras se cargaban de reflejos sobre mis ojos abiertos' (195-96). Here we find Andrea's preferred position: to be swept along by the current. As she says, she is 'acostumbrada a dejar que la corriente de los acontecimientos me arrastrase por sí misma' (255). Indeed, she seems to derive feelings of safety and a kind of primal, infantile pleasure from being immersed, lost in the crowd, being 'una gota entre la corriente' (11), 'un elemento más, pequeño y perdido en ella' (225). In short, she finds her greatest satisfactions in experiencing a loss of identity, in merging into something else, in abandoning the contours of the self. So, as well as acting as a stimulus to a new awareness, as Thompson suggests, it could be argued that the water imagery in *Nada* also indicates the precise opposite: it conjures up a symbolic, illusory space where problems and pressures disappear, identities dissolve and where the protagonist experiences those regressive, babyish 'oceanic feelings' of contentment and mystical emotion.[7] Also, in its function as a cleansing, purgative agent, water is clearly used to assuage and remove the taint of sensuality which Andrea often feels and regards as improper in one so young and immature. For example, having been accused by Juan of having multiple lovers and likened to a dog (i.e. a whore) on the city streets, Andrea becomes extremely nervous, perhaps even titillated, at a view which corresponds in her imagination to her alter ego, her dark side. In order to alleviate her anxiety, she takes a shower, but 'El agua [...] me parecía tibia, incapaz de refrescar mi carne ni de limpiarla' (199-200). The water fails to refresh and comfort, fails to purge Andrea's flesh because she, in her fantasy, regards herself as a tainted woman. She plays with the idea of being a whore, a thought which both excites her imagination and, at the same time, makes her feel guilty. Hence, the ritual act of taking a shower, a symbolic means of washing away the imputation of sinfulness and regaining that primal state of purity and innocence. If, as I have suggested, water imagery is suggestive of escape, fusion, non-identity and mystical reverie, the same might be said of the novel's obsessive concern with art, artistic processes and artistic creativity.

Several critics have acknowledged the importance of art in *Nada* (6, 10, 28). They note how the narrator relates to the world around her mainly through her sensory awareness and how this derives from her experience of the visual and spatial arts, which is then re-elaborated in writing. The process of literary reconstruction

---

[7] On the notion of 'oceanic feelings', see the relevant entry in Charles Rycroft's *A Critical Dictionary of Psychoanalysis* (Harmondsworth: Penguin, 1968), p.105.

of the narrator's memories, which become the text of the novel, is
thus heavily indebted to the influence of art. Indeed, art in different
forms is to be found everywhere in the novel. Many of the characters
engage in artistic activities of one sort or another. At Aribau, Román
is a consummate painter and musician; Juan, by contrast, is his
mediocre, talentless counterpart; Gloria acts as nude model for her
husband; at Vía Layetana, Ena's mother is an accomplished pianist
and singer; Jaime is an architect; and apart from Pons, Andrea's
young male friends are all involved in artistic pursuits: Yturdiaga has
completed a four volume novel and seeks a publisher; Guíxols is
already established as a painter of seascapes and Pujol aspires to
painterly status. Andrea herself, of course, is the budding writer,
desperate to tell the story of Aribau and to enjoy the 'encanto de
vestir todo esto con hipótesis fantásticas en largas conversaciones'
(63).

     The language of the novel is also heavily influenced by various
artistic styles. As Roberta Johnson has shown, the narrator trans-
forms novelistic reality into art using two dominant and clearly
recognizable styles, which correspond to the binary organization of
the novel (*6*, p.58). On the one hand, we find Expressionism, which
is used to portray the novel's dark side, its uncanny, Gothic
atmospheres and the forces of decay and death; these are most
evident in the opening chapter, the descent into the *barrio gótico* and
the scenes at Aribau, near the end of the novel, after Román's
suicide. Here the emphasis is on evoking lugubrious, stifling rooms,
dim lighting, ghostly apparitions, physical deformity, ugliness,
madness and death. There is also a possible hint of Surrealism in the
way Andrea presents some of her dreams and nightmares, particularly the strange transformation of the hospital scene involving Juan
and Gloria into the castle scene with Román (56). On the other hand,
we find the luminosity of Impressionism, especially in Andrea's
Sunday visits to the beach with Jaime and Ena, in the studio of the
young artists 'lleno de luz' (154), and at the wharf (254). Here,
obviously, darkness gives way to light, evil to goodness, the
unfamiliar and negative to the familiar and positive. Generally, the
atmospheres and colorations conjure up not uncertainty and dread,

but contentment, friendship, oneness with nature and a certain mystical union with larger cosmic forces. For example, in the towering façade of the Cathedral, Andrea finds 'una armonía severa' (116), 'Una paz, una imponente claridad' (116). Like Román's music or the contemplation of the idealized lovers, Jaime and Ena (139), the Cathedral engulfs the protagonist, sweeping her into a reverie, suspending time: 'Dejé que aquel profundo hechizo de las formas me penetrara durante unos minutos' (116). This gives us a clear indication of the nature and purpose of the narrator's interest in art.

Johnson has argued that art in *Nada* 'provides a soothing, contemplative calm, a permanent reality in opposition to the passion and flux of human relationships' (*6*, p.64). This certainly seems to be the case, as Andrea confirms when contrasting the aesthetically-satisfying closure of a novel or film to the relativity of life, in which 'todo sigue, se hace gris, se arruina viviendo' (251). Life is subject to a process of decay while art, especially in its classical forms, is seen as unchanging and permanent. Art thus seems to provide an escape from the ravages of time into a region where all is whole and secure. However, as Ruth El Saffar has pointed out, though the narrator of *Nada* tries to disengage life from time through art, art is incapable of arresting the forces of degeneration (*10*, p.127). In this sense, writing the text of *Nada* is no solution to the possible difficulties or crisis in which the older, Madrid-based, Andrea finds herself. The act of writing is only a temporary respite and escape from the flux of existence, a consoling fiction. What neither Johnson nor El Saffar indicates, however, is that art and architecture act as a means of sublimation for Andrea's libidinal drives, which, like those of Román, include a desire for self-annihilation. Contemplating the Cathedral, at the end of the novel, Andrea experiences a feeling of 'belleza casi mística. Como un deseo de morirme allí [...] mirando hacia arriba [...] Y me dolió el pecho de hambre y de deseos inconfesables, al respirar' (287). In this act of mystical contemplation, Andrea, 'entontecida y medio estática' (287), 'medio loca' (288) expresses a desire for an imaginary state of oneness, for a place which precedes the relativity and flux of ordinary existence and guarantees permanence, i.e. a symbolic death. Art offers this realm of unity, harmony and stability, this fairy land behind the mirror, even though it is no more than a fantasy. This brings me to one of the most important features of the novel which so far has received relatively little critical attention: the function and importance of the gaze.

In *Nada*, references to mirrors, glasses, reflecting surfaces, eyes and the gaze, both literal and metaphorical, are extremely numerous. For example, on arriving at Aribau, Andrea is unable to tell which balconies correspond to her step-parents' flat: 'Los miré y no pude adivinar cuáles serían' (13). Almost immediately, for the protagonist, her own eyes simply register confusion and uncertainty: 'Todo empezaba a ser extraño a mi imaginación' (13). Once inside Aribau, her confusion is compounded by the unnerving gaze of others. Her first contact with Angustias, taller than her, is to be forced to look into her reproachful eyes: 'me obligó a mirarla así' (15); Gloria stares at Andrea: 'me miraba sonriendo, abobada por el sueño' (16). With her step-family now assembled: 'Los ojos se abrían asombrados sobre mí. Los ojos de Angustias y de todos los demás' (17). Andrea's first experience of Aribau is to be positioned as the object of external scrutiny; she is made to feel extremely nervous and takes refuge in a shower: '¡Qué alivio estar fuera de las miradas de aquellos seres originales!' (17). In the filthy bathroom, we find the first reference to mirrors, in which the cobweb-covered ceiling is reflected, though not Andrea's body. Shortly after, Andrea relieves her terror by looking at the stars through the open balcony, 'al verlas tuve unas ganas súbitas de llorar, como si viera amigos antiguos bruscamente recobrados' (19). This introduces a repeated feature, the searching gaze of the protagonist, which finds relief from anxiety through contemplation of an open prospect or vista, e.g. the sea, the sky, the stars, the Cathedral. The following morning, Andrea wakes up to find her grandmother looking at her, but it is a youthful figure and not the ghostly apparition of the previous night (21). Only later is it revealed that the grandmother as well as the grandfather are merely figures in a portrait, which Andrea has been contemplating and which triggers her daydreams concerning the prehistory of Aribau.

In the first ten pages of the novel, as can be appreciated, references to eyes, reflective surfaces and the gaze are legion and broadly suggest a transformation of the familiar into the unfamiliar. What Andrea sees does not correspond to her memory or imagination. The reality she thought she would encounter at Aribau has somehow been overturned, dislocated. A stable and harmonious past, symbolized by the portrait of the grandparents, is now in disarray and is signalled in Andrea's many references to her own confusion, turmoil, insecurity, etc. She literally cannot believe her eyes and eyes become the focal point of her many apprehensions. Moreover, at the very beginning of the novel, Andrea becomes the object of the gaze of her step-family, a gaze which is both reproachful and oppressive, which penetrates to her very core and produces deep feelings of anxiety and guilt. One of Andrea's major problems in this regard is that when she makes eye contact with other characters her gaze is not one of power and self-confidence, but of weakness and impotence, as Gloria reveals: 'Pero no me mires así, no me mires así, Andrea, que me das muchas ganas de reír esa cara que pones' (107). Young Pons mentions the same thing (60), as does Ena: 'Tenías los ojos brillantes y andabas torpe, abstraída, sin fijarte en nada... Nos reíamos de ti' (163).

Andrea develops a phobia about eyes, experiencing unnecessary anxiety out of all proportion to the threat posed. In her dreams, she finds the threatening, censoring eyes of Angustias and Román staring directly at her, fixing her, possessing her, nailing her down. In her waking hours, this phobia is just as apparent in her encounters with the beggar, whom Angustias had adopted as a symbol of her charity and good nature. His suppliant look severely disturbs the protagonist, who is obsessively aware of his eyes: 'a veces los ojos se le escapaban' (185), 'sus ojos se disparaban hacia mí' (185), 'Los ojos suyos seguían chispeando' (185), 'su saludo y sus ojos bailarines me perseguían, me obsesionaban en aquel trocito de la calle' (186). The solution to her problem, Andrea muses, is to be looked at in a very different way, to be discovered, admired and made to feel wonderful: 'Tal vez el sentido de la vida para una mujer consiste únicamente en ser descubierta así, mirada de manera que ella misma se sienta

irradiante de luz' (215). Pons has already tried to tell Andrea, in
words and looks, that he considers her pretty (215). However,
Andrea's difficulty is that she cannot imagine herself as an attractive
woman, as a credible object of masculine desire. She is aware of her
own desire, but refuses to acknowledge her own desirability. Hence
the disaster of Pons's party, where she retreats into her self-
deprecating role of 'plain Jane'. Andrea claims that she wants
independence and to be like Ena. However, to be equal with the
male, female desire has to be active and actively gazing. Ena
achieves this, operating as a seer as well as the object of another's
eyes. Andrea, however, is unable to gaze actively, unable to assert
her desire as legitimate. Thus she is always in a subordinate position,
always prey to the threatening look of others. She finds safety and a
degree of satisfaction only at a distance, in the furtive gaze of the
voyeur and by extension, in that of the writer.

The operation of the gaze is closely related to that of mirrors
and reflective surfaces. Traditionally, in novel writing and particularly in Gothic fiction, mirrors open up an indeterminate area, where
reflected images of the self begin to slide away and where distortions
and deformations are the norm. Mirrors produce distance and a
different space where notions of the stable self undergo transforma-
tions. Mirrors act as metaphors for the production of other selves, of
doubles, the reflection in the glass being the subject's other. In short,
mirror images are used to suggest the instability of the real and the
fluidity of the self. At the same time, they also offer the illusion of
wholeness and coincidence with the subject's self-image. In this
connection, a striking feature of *Nada* is the way many of the
characters seek confirmation of their own self-image in others, i.e.
others are called upon to act as mirrors. For example, Gloria repeatedly asks Andrea to confirm just how beautiful a body she has (35).
Gloria's childish vanity is an expression of her healthy narcissism
and she has no inhibitions in regarding her own body as a desirable
object. Román is also intensely narcissistic, yet his self-love is sick
and perverted and prevents him from making healthy emotional
attachments. Also, such is his investment in his own ego that he
continually seeks, indeed demands, reinforcement and indulgence

from others, which is usually forthcoming. He initially thinks he has found in Andrea someone very like himself: wild, cruel and perverse, an image which Andrea prefers not to disrupt; indeed, because of her inferiority complex, she colludes in confirming it: 'No me gustaba desilusionarle porque vagamente yo me sentía inferior' (39). Angustias offers another variant of childish narcissism. She regards herself as the reference point around which Aribau is organized and without which it cannot function. Where Román thinks he controls everyone in the flat downstairs, Angustias believes herself to be indispensable to the maintenance of Aribau's bourgeois morality and traditional values. Both characters suffer from a perverted sense of their self-importance and there is little evidence of a healthy self-esteem, except in the case of Gloria. In *Nada*, then, we find examples of the way characters act as mirrors which seem to reflect the illusion of the self and confirm the egocentrism of others. But we also find cases where the image of the self becomes distorted, where it slides, begins to dissolve or appears as an absence.

In chapter 1 of the novel, we find the first mention of mirrors: Andrea takes a shower and in the mirror situated over the wash basin 'se reflejaba el bajo techo cargado de telas de arañas' (17). What is not mentioned as being reflected, however, is Andrea's body. Rather, it is surrounded by a protective cascade of 'hilos brillantes de agua' (17). The body thus appears to be an absence. Initially, Andrea is a figure without an identity. In the long wardrobe mirror in Angustias's room, Andrea sees 'de refilón, la imagen de mis dieciocho años áridos encerrados en una figura alargada' (103). Here, it seems that Andrea sees herself in precisely the same way she regarded the inhabitants of Aribau on her arrival: '[...] figuras [...] alargadas y sombrías. Alargadas, quietas y tristes [...]' (15). It is as if she were taking on their appearance, succumbing to the enervating effects of disease-ridden Aribau. Later, feeling extremely depressed after Pons's party, Andrea recalls seeing something in Angustias's mirror: 'vi que [...] estaba toda mi habitación llena de un color de seda gris y allí mismo, una larga sombra. Me acerqué y el espectro se acercó conmigo. Al fin, alcancé a ver mi propia cara desdibujada sobre el

camisón de hilo [...] Era una rareza estarme contemplando así, casi
sin verme, con los ojos abiertos' (213-14). Here, the protagonist's
self-confidence and sense of identity are in severe trouble. As she
raises her hand to touch her face, her features seem to slide away:
'parecían escapárseme' (215). This apparent dissolution of the self
responds to Andrea's experience at Pons's party, where her long-held
dream of seeing herself transformed into a beautiful princess —
'precisamente rubia, como describían los cuentos' (215) — is
shattered and reversed. Significantly, the process of reversal is begun
by Pons's mother and 'la mirada suya, indefinible, dirigida a mis
viejos zapatos' (218). Distressed by what she interprets as a
censoring gaze, Andrea's anxiety increases as she sees herself in a
mirror: 'blanca y gris, deslucida entre los alegres trajes de verano que
me rodeaban. Absolutamente seria entre la animación de todos y me
sentí un poco ridícula' (219). Interestingly, Andrea's worn-out shoes
are contrasted with Yturdiaga's glistening footwear: 'unos zapatos
brillantes como espejos' (220), in which Andrea again sees reflected
her inferiority. She sees in the mirror and in reflective objects
distorted images which reflect her subjective state and particularly
her anxieties about being plain, poorly-dressed and uninteresting.
Near the end of the novel, after Román's suicide, Andrea takes
another shower: 'En el espejo, me encontré reflejada, misera-
blemente flaca y con los dientes chocándome' (278). Here, as she
tries to wash away her imagined responsibility for Román's death, it
is clear that Aribau has taken its toll. Andrea sees herself as an
emaciated, wasted figure, but also 'histérica' 'idiotizada' (278),
numbed by the tragedy. There follows a period of mourning for
Román, during which she experiences 'extrañas visiones' (283) and
sees in the mirror, not her full body but only 'un trozo de mi propio
cuerpo' (285). Is this the mature, self-confident, independent Andrea
mentioned by many of the critics or might it indicate a body and
moreover a psyche in fragments? Unlike Gloria, whose reflection in
the mirror simply confirms her view of herself as pretty and
desirable, Andrea is too self-deprecatory, too masochistic, too afraid
to express her desiring side and see herself as an object of desire. In
Andrea's case, the mirror and its substitutes throw up images which

reflect her fearful, repressed side and in so doing, perhaps betray the shadow of Angustias, whose repressions Andrea seems to have internalized.

So far, this chapter has concentrated on aspects of imagery, foreshadowing and the various dominant motifs in the novel, but less so on those stylistic features one would normally associate with a first-person narrative. Typically, in a story where the narrator tells the reader now about events that happened then and where the outcome of those events is known, many possibilities arise for exploiting within the narrative such resources as irony, satire and humour. However, Laforet chooses not to explore these possibilities to any great extent, though it is slightly unfair to claim, as Yates does, that Laforet 'evades or possibly systematically eliminates this potential of her narrative form' (*31*, p.15). Though there is little evidence of satire or humour in the novel, we do find some instances of verbal irony, where a surface statement is undercut or reversed by other clues in the text. For example, when the narrator refers to Gloria as 'la mujer serpiente' (104), she is clearly ironizing Angustias's attitude to Gloria as intruder and cause of Aribau's fall. When Andrea refers to entering a 'vida nueva', it soon becomes apparent that this is not the case. When she talks of the imminent struggle with Angustias in terms of 'una tempestad inevitable' (59), the fact is that the struggle never comes. There may be heavy, unintended irony in Juan's words of advice to Andrea before her departure: 'Ya verás cómo, de todas maneras, vivir en casa extraña no es lo mismo que estar con tu familia' (293), as if family life at Aribau had been in any way satisfactory and blood ties were more important than other sorts of relationship. Also, there is the possibly ironic application of the Homeric quotation to the 'bohemios': 'Demos gracias al cielo que valemos infinitamente más que nuestros antepasados-Homero' (159), at which Andrea is prompted to laugh. However, where Andrea the narrator might have taken the opportunity to satirize the arrogance and artistic pretensions of these 'hijos de papá', she does not do so to any great extent, largely because she feels 'muy divertida y contenta' (158) in their company. Her barbs are limited to details such as Pujol's dress and dirty ears:

'El único mal vestido y con las orejas sucias era Pujol' (156) or to the
fact that Pons was 'hijo único y muy mimado' (156). The main
instances of ironic critique seem to be reserved for the protagonist
herself, who is the object of the narrator's self-mockery and self-
deprecation. For example, the narrator reflects bitterly on the stupidity and naivety of her childish illusions: 'En realidad, mi pena de
chiquilla desilusionada no merecía tanto aparato [...] A mi lado,
dolores más grandes me habían dejado indiferente hasta la burla'
(224). At Pons's party, Andrea is also aware of her own ineptitude
and tactlessness: '¿Es posible que sea yo — pensé — la protagonista
de tan ridícula escena? [...] ¿Por qué digo tal cantidad de idioteces?'
(222).

Apart from the above rather random examples, perhaps the
most important instance of irony is the title of the novel itself, a title
which has never ceased to invite speculation among readers and
critics. Laforet's choice of such a word for her title may have
responded to her own retiring view of her work as of little value or
inconsequential. Whatever the personal motivations for the choice,
the word 'nada' obviously signifies something, the negative suggests
a positive. At the very least, it refers to the text the reader has before
her, an object or artefact which constitutes a re-elaboration of
Andrea's memories of her year at Aribau. As she points out, 'De la
casa de la calle de Aribau, no me llevaba nada. Al menos, así creía
yo entonces' (294). Since then, of course, things have changed. She
may not have found happiness, fulfilment, love or Mr Right at
Aribau, but she does take something with her, whose importance she
realizes only later. This is her store of memories, which she feels
compelled to revise and revisit in the writing process. 'Nada', in this
sense, refers to the artistic creativity involved in the re-writing
process and by implication, it relates to the aesthetic experience of
the reader in the act of consuming the text. The reading process may
be nothing in itself, but on reflection, it may yield unforeseen
possibilities of meaning. Relatedly, 'nada' has to do with the poetic
fragment which prefaces the text and, as mentioned at the beginning
of this chapter, with the way in which we gain experience. The
fragment stresses the importance of the senses in registering and

reading the world and the way the brute facts of empirical experience constitute 'realidades fijas', revealing the unexpected truth of reality. Curiously and perhaps ironically, *Nada* as a literary artefact is notable, not for its direct, unmediated transcription of post-war Spanish reality through sensory perception, but for its literariness, its active, self-conscious indulgence in literary re-elaboration. Sensory perception is far from being unmediated, therefore, as Laforet seems to claim. It is already organized by previous experience and frames of reference into which new experience is slotted, sorted and re-elaborated. If *Nada* tells us anything about gaining experience, it is that experience is already mediated, never direct, already resonant with meanings and nuances and, as the present novel shows, already indebted to previous modes of making sense through reading and writing.

Another very important meaning suggested by the novel's title is, of course, 'nothingness', by which I do not refer to Existentialist notions of 'néant', i.e. a region, uninfluenced by a God or transcendent force, in which man is forced to choose and to commit himself and where authentic existence is possible. In relation to *Nada*, 'nothingness' refers to something very different. It has to do with the way the protagonist is unable to let her defences down when faced with male sexuality, but is happy to be swept along and transported into a mystical, cosmic realm — a 'nada' — through aesthetic experience. On numerous occasions, through the contemplation of a painting, a building, a street or even Ena and Jaime, Andrea merges emotionally and psychologically with the object of sight. Such scenes act as a medium or conduit through which the protagonist can cast off her daily anxieties and find solace and contentment. Listening to Román's music, for example, she remarks: '[...] yo cambiaba completamente. Desaparecían mis reservas [...] Mi alma recibía el sonido como una lluvia la tierra áspera' (41). Andrea cannot verbalize what the music means to her: '¿Qué te dice la música?', asks Román, to which she replies 'Nada, no sé, sólo me gusta [...] Nada' (41). At this lack of critical appreciation, Román is most disappointed. But the power of music to evoke harmony, beauty, stability and happiness is so great that it allows Andrea to transcend

the divisions and contradictions of life and experience 'un anegarse
en la nada. Mi propia muerte, el sentimiento de mi desesperación
hecha belleza, angustiosa armonía sin luz' (41). In this rather
metaphysical 'nada', the splits, separations, fragmentations, divisions
and lacks which the protagonist feels at different moments in her life
are all smoothed over and resolved. The binary organization of the
novel, its oppositions between good and evil, decorum and desire
and all those forces which create tension and contradiction are
overcome. Here, 'nothingness' suggests an area lying before and
beyond the flux and inevitable decay of ordinary existence, a region
which fulfils desires and which makes people feel happy and safe, a
fairy land, an uncorrupted world. In this connection, Angustias refers
to Aribau before Gloria's arrival as 'el paraíso' which has been
destroyed by 'la serpiente maligna' (102). In a sense, Andrea returns
to Aribau hoping to experience it as she did when she was seven
years old, as a childhood paradise. In other words, a further meaning
of 'nothingness' has to do with an edenic realm of innocence and
security, a yearning for wholeness, fullness of being, identity,
origins, a return to the primordial family where all is sweetness and
light. In the language of psychoanalysis, this region is commonly
known as the 'imaginary'. The word describes the stage before a
child separates itself from the mother and enters the 'symbolic order',
the area of language and social development. The imaginary thus
refers to a state of unity with the mother, of undifferentiation, of
non-being, a paradise which is lost by the fall into socialization and
growing up. Andrea's many references to feeling 'arrastrada', to
being immersed in and totally absorbed by aesthetic experience, to
losing her sense of self and experiencing a form of symbolic death
— all these relate to this meaning of 'nothingness', a code word for
the imaginary, for paradise. As a literary text, *Nada* constitutes an
imaginative return to Aribau, a return through the literary re-
elaboration of memories. At the same time, the text describes a
powerful desire directed towards a further return, a return to a pre-
Oedipal fantasy land, replete with dark princes and blond heroines
and inspired by children's stories. Again, in perhaps vulgar
psychoanalytical terms, these returns speak of a desire to journey

back to the warmth and safety of the maternal breast or even the watery paradise of the maternal womb. To conclude, the irony of *Nada* is that it is a something (a text, an artefact) which expresses an underlying desire in the protagonist to become nothing, to plunge ('nadar') into 'la inconsciencia absoluta' (159). Of course, as she is overwhelmingly aware, such a return to a childhood paradise is no more than a fantasy, but no less powerful, attractive and thrilling for being impossible.

6. Sources, Influences, Genre

A number of attempts have been made to classify *Nada* and to suggest various sources from which Laforet may have drawn her literary inspiration. Though not written to a formula, there is no doubt that *Nada* draws heavily on other writers and narrative types, although it may not be possible to say exactly how and from which ones. It is now fairly widely accepted that, in its first-person narrative perspective and its characterization, Laforet's novel is indebted to the influence of the nineteenth-century English novel, particularly Dickens and the work of the Brontës, including *Jane Eyre*, *Wuthering Heights* and perhaps even *Shirley* and *Villette*. Also, as Johnson has pointed out, certain moments in the novel where Andrea contemplates a scene and draws general conclusions about life are reminiscent of a technique used by Marcel Proust, in particular in his *A l'ombre des jeunes filles en fleur* (*6*, p.59). As regards the treatment of the house at Aribau and the evocation of its Gothic atmospheres, there are strong reminiscences of Dickens and perhaps Edgar Allen Poe's *The Fall of the House of Usher*. Relatedly, Laforet's interest in split personalities and other selves probably indicates a knowledge of some of Dostoevsky's schizophrenic character creations such as Golyadkin in *The Double* or Ivan in *The Brothers Karamazov* and perhaps Robert Louis Stevenson's *The Strange Case of Dr Jekyll and Mr Hyde*.

It has been suggested that, given its title, its time of writing and its proximity to the publication of Sartre's *L'Être et le Néant* (1943), *Nada* somehow shares the existentialist concerns of its French counterpart and can thus be linked to a wider European

Existentialist movement.[8] This linkage, I should argue, is mistaken. The title of Laforet's novel was both an unusual and a highly opportune choice, in its time, but as she herself pointed out, it was most probably made because of her personal attitude towards her work: 'Porque a mí me parece nada; porque lo que escribí era nada.'[9] There is little or nothing in the novel which would seriously connect it to the philosophical concerns of the French movement (man's alienation in a hostile world, hell as others, the individual condemned to freedom, the burden of free choice, etc.). Indeed, the linkage seems just as gratuitous as the one regularly made between Camus's *L'Étranger* (1942) and Cela's *La familia de Pascual Duarte* (1942), on the basis that they were published in the same year and that Meursault's killing of the Arab supposedly parallels the Chispa episode. There is a connection, however, between Laforet's work and Cela's notorious novel. It is one to which *Nada* has been frequently compared and with which it does have certain similarities (see *31*). *La familia de Pascual Duarte* has usually been seen as the initiator of a type of literature, in vogue in the 1940s, which took inordinate pleasure in describing the most sordid, repulsive and violent aspects of human behaviour. I refer, of course, to Tremendismo, a trend which had significant antecedents in Spanish artistic life in the Picaresque, Quevedo, Goya and in the turn-of-the-century *esperpento*. Also, in its post-1939 version, it was a trend which to some extent represented a purging of the horrors of the Civil War but also acted as a safety valve for the many repressions imposed on social and cultural life in the 1940s.

Glorifying a racial primitivism and a tender yet terrifying Hispanic machismo, *La familia de Pascual Duarte* placed extraordinary emphasis on sex, violence, brutality, murder, sadism, psychological trauma and death. But it did so in ways which combined a highly lyrical, literary style with a view of life reduced to its barest, most elemental, biological determinants. That particular

[8] Pedro Laín Entralgo, *ABC* (13 Jan. 1946); Gonzalo Sobejano, *Novela española de nuestro tiempo (en busca del pueblo perdido)* (Madrid: Castalia, 1975), p.145.

[9] Carmen Laforet, *La Estafeta Literaria* (25 Sept. 1945); Sobejano, p.146.

combination of 'ternura' and 'estilo brutal' are borrowed and recycled, I should argue, in *Nada*. This is most vividly expressed in the two brothers, in Román's sadism and also in Juan's psychopathic behaviour. Juan is to some extent a Pascual figure, tender and gentle on some occasions, but abnormally aggressive and brutal on others and prone to venting his frustrations and inferiority complex through wife-beating and violent rages. For example, during the incident of the 'pañuelo', in a typical outburst, there is 'un bofetón de Juan, tan brutal, que hizo tambalearse a Angustias y caer al suelo' (73). However, towards his baby, 'Juan tenía para la criatura ternuras insospechadas, íntimas y casi feroces' (98). A further similarity between the novels is that the narrative technique of *La familia de Pascual Duarte* is based on the conventions of the epistolary novel and confessional literature. Now while *Nada* does not exploit the Celian devices of the fictional editor or the various letters which enclose the unusually articulate written record of Pascual, the novels have in common the intention to open the self up to scrutiny, to reveal the past and to seek some form of understanding or absolution. It is this confessional impulse found in both novels which has been somewhat overlooked in *Nada* and whose elucidation might help extend the generic boundaries within which the novel has traditionally been read.

A feature which is virtually synonymous with any first-person narration is that of self-exposure. Pascual Duarte engages in a 'pública confesión', as he declares to Barrera López. Since hers is a rather more private and intimate matter, Andrea is obviously far more circumspect. But even so, confession is an important motif in *Nada* and an activity in which many of the characters engage in one form or another. For example, the Abuela attends Mass and confession on a regular basis and even feels compelled to seek forgiveness for the little fibs she tells Jerónimo Sanz in order to prevent him from locating Angustias (82). Angustias is also obsessed by her religious observances but for rather different reasons. Apart from supervising Andrea's devotions and checking on the choice of dress of the parishioners (107), she uses attendance at church as a way of secretly meeting Sanz. Significantly, immediately after bringing their relationship to an end, she departs 'para confesarse en una iglesia cercana' (83). Apart from these straightforward examples of religious or ritual confession, we find other more indirect forms. At several moments in the novel, Andrea is inclined to regard other characters as longing to pour out their hearts to her and feels excited at being chosen as a listening post. In fact, she actively engages in a form of wish-fulfilment, over-reading the desire of others to talk and unburden themselves. For example, she sees Román as 'desesperado' (86), anxious to confide: 'En realidad me parecía que le hacía yo verdadera falta, que le hacía verdadera falta hablar, como me había dicho. Tal vez quería confesarse conmigo; arrepentirse delante de mí o justificarse' (88). Since Andrea finds it so difficult to speak herself, she is an avid listener and, as we have seen, longs to indulge in 'el tono misterioso y reticente de las confidencias' (59). This she does on several important occasions, with Gloria, Margarita and Ena, who all feel a need to unlock the cupboard and reveal their secrets. Or so it seems. On the surface, *Nada* becomes a veritable confessional space.

What of the content of these confessions? Invariably, they have to do with illicit passions, disruptive desire, guilt at bodily longings, hunger for human contact and so on. Gloria, for example, reveals to Andrea that she was in love with Román and would have left Juan for him, even though she knew she was carrying Juan's baby (206). Margarita tells Andrea that, even after her year of exile in the country away from Román, on her return to the city, 'cada árbol, cada gota de luz [...] me traía su olor, hasta dilatarme las narices presintiéndolo' (236). Despite her fears, Ena becomes 'obsesionada por Román [...] intoxicada', gripped by 'el dualismo de fuerzas que me impulsan' (266) and absorbed by 'el juego apasionante en que se convertía aquello para mí' (267). In similar fashion, Ena's mother reveals how she became infected by Román's infantile cruelty and found herself enjoying punishing her husband just as Román had tormented her: 'Por una vez, comprendía el placer que había hecho vibrar el alma de Román al mortificarme' (238). In bed with Gloria, Andrea experiences an irresistible desire for bodily contact: 'estaba unida a Gloria por el feroz deseo de mi organismo' (132).

In a word, these women confess their sexuality, a sexuality which has largely been repressed, which is curiously infantile and sadistic and which has its darker side: compulsive voyeurism, hints of lesbianism, sadomasochism, etc. Predictably perhaps, the dark side of female sexuality is shown to be unlocked and activated by the seductive charms of the male, principally Román. However, the male characters do not emerge as victors in this battle of the sexes. Juan, for example, is unable to assert a confident male identity and is in some ways feminized. He disintegrates emotionally after Román's death and the manner of his mourning reveals a very powerful, latent, homoerotic attachment: 'el dolor de Juan era ímpudico, enloquecedor, como el de una mujer por su amante' (281). It is also worth noting that, even if they wish to do so, the main male characters are unable to engage seriously in confessional activity. By the end of the novel, Román has still not found someone who will listen to his story and attempt to understand him. Partly because of this, he commits suicide and as a result, his doting brother goes mad. It is never strongly suggested in the novel, but Román's suicide is arguably linked to his inability to establish normal heterosexual relations, an inability which very likely stems from his own repressed homosexual feelings.

Judging by the fate of main male characters, it would seem that the act of confession is regarded by Laforet as profoundly therapeutic, a necessary release of repressed anxiety and guilty feelings and thus to be encouraged, since it does one good. As Michel Foucault has argued, however, to speak of sexuality, to respond to the injunction to 'let it all hang out', represents its control. A strategy of self-exposure thus implicitly carries within it a strategy of self-containment. Foucault regards confession as the modern organization of sexuality into verbal discourse, particularly its aberrant forms.[10] Its major function will be to prohibit certain deviant sexual practices, uphold heterosexual relations and at the

---

[10] Michel Foucault, *The History of Sexuality*, I, trans. R. Hurley (London: Allen Lane, 1979), p.62.

same time promise to exonerate, redeem and purify the speaker. (As noted in a previous chapter, *Nada* is characterized by a powerful undercurrent to absolve women from any imputation of sin or excess carnality; this drive towards innocence and purity is symbolized perhaps in 'las bellas palabras del Ave María' (171), that is, the song to the Virgin, the pure mother, recited by Andrea.) Laforet's novel is thus in some ways comparable to the Church confessional. It explores predominantly female sexuality, recommends that all be revealed, emphasizes the therapeutic value of the exercise and also the pleasure involved in it, particularly for the listener. Above all, the novel suggests that to control aberrant sexuality, one must tell of it, one must identify the source of temptation, expose it and reject it. On a wider front, the novel suggests that to confirm the truth and propriety of bourgeois morality and family relations, one must reveal their underside: illicit sexual relations, crumbling marriages, problems of inheritance, duty and allegiance.

Paradoxically, while *Nada* presents the act of confession as both emotionally satisfying and highly therapeutic, it also shows it to be an act of dissimulation and non-revelation. As we have already seen, in her role as first-person narrator Andrea reveals remarkably little about herself. Her views are always provisional, relative, cautious and uncertain. Her sexuality is largely silent, coy, reserved, only expressed through the body in fevers, hallucinations, dreams, and lived out in other characters — in short, her sexual drives are vicariously fulfilled through substitutes. Her silence is also a counterweight to the garrulousness of other characters. Unable to voice her desires, she sublimates them through literary fantasies, which function as projections of her bodily longings. These sublimations compensate for society's prohibitions by allowing some degree of vicarious fulfilment of unruly libidinal energy. The confession motif in *Nada* is a channel for this energy, it expresses an urge to tell of, but also a requirement to control, sexuality and in the end to reaffirm the institutional order. The confession may be seen then as a placebo, an activity which brings out all the thrills and anxieties of owning up to the pleasures of the flesh, but which helps to neutralize the urge to transgress. Within the narrative, Andrea as actor is in the position of the listener, the recipient of the confessions of others, but engaged at a distance, from behind the metaphorical partition of the confessional. Likewise the reader occupies Andrea's detached position of spectator and like her reinforces the powerful voyeuristic impulse in the novel by colluding in overhearing, spying and listening in to the stories of others. The reader is invited to share the pleasures of the confessional space, the revelations concerning the dark side of sexual activity, but also to recognise that marriage, children and the family are the required antidote to disruptive desire and the temptations of the flesh.

The above comments on the confessional impulse in *Nada* relate to the wider question of how we might describe the novel in generic terms. To date, as noted in chapter 4, *Nada* has been classified predominantly as a *Bildungsroman*, a novel of maturation from childhood to adulthood, based on several stages of development. Within this generally-accepted framework, critics have proposed various narrative types to which *Nada* might be compared. Foster, for example, links it with medieval romance and Gothic fiction, stressing its stock characters, situations and settings, but perhaps undervaluing its psychological and ideological concerns (*13*). Villegas compares it to the narrative structure of folk tales and quest stories, showing how it lends itself to archetypal and mythic interpretations (*30*). Other critics, such as Elizabeth Ordóñez, Sara Schyfter and Margaret Jones, writing from various feminist perspectives, emphazise the repressive aspects of traditional family relations, male sexuality and the reintegration of the protagonist into patriarchal society (*22, 24, 18*). In chapter 4, I attempted to address some of the main points raised by these and other critics concerning the dominant view of *Nada* as a novel of female development. In the following considerations, I should like to suggest a further sub-generic framework for reading the novel, one which relates to the notion of confession and which might extend and enrich already established modes of classification. Briefly, I wish to consider *Nada* in terms of a literature of desire.

Nada is clearly a nostalgic novel. The primary impulse in the eighteen-year-old protagonist is to look back to a lost world of childhood innocence, security and stability, a lost moral and social hierarchy — a 'paradise lost' which the novel attempts to recapture by negative example. The attempt to return to this world through writing and thus compensate for a loss or lack in the present may be understood in terms of a literature of desire. As Rosemary Jackson has argued, a literature of desire is one which seeks to recover that which is experienced as absence or loss.[11] Moreover, desire operates in two related ways: it can be told of and it can be expelled, especially when it is a destabilizing force which threatens the social and cultural order. Both these functions can be fulfilled at the same time, i.e. desire can be expelled by having been told about. *Nada*, it seems to me, is a good example of a literature which is concerned with the re-experiencing of desire through writing and its subsequent containment and expulsion.

By desire, we can mean various things: a series of pictures we construct of the world, which may be inaccurate or illusory; an area of repressed activity, a taboo; an appetite or an activity directed towards a lack or an absence. All of these features could be applied to *Nada* in various ways. To mention just one, it is clear that the emphasis on physical hunger in the novel, on food and its substitutes (especially in Juan's lugubrious still-life paintings), on 'caprichos' which are only rarely satisfied (Andrea's taste for expensive sweets, flowers, cigarettes), are extended metaphors for other sorts of unsatisfied desires, for emotional and sexual needs which have been denied or repressed. Also, the notion of desire has implications for the way we regard the nature of the self. It calls into question the idea that *Nada* is fundamentally concerned with Andrea's personal maturation into a fully-fledged, independent, human subject. The point is that desire, a search in pursuit of a lack, leads to the break-up of the self into its others, into a series of partial selves or disguises which, in *Nada*, are projected onto and fulfilled in other characters. For example, the act of narration, of revisiting the past in writing, is an occasion which allows the older Andrea to re-invent herself in multiple versions, to find odd bits of herself in Román, Ena,

---

[11] Rosemary Jackson, *Fantasy. The Literature of Subversion* (London: Methuen, 1981), p.3.

Angustias, the grandmother etc. The purpose of re-experiencing the past, then, may not be to confirm the permanence of the stable, identical self, but to re-release the energies of the prospective self or selves, which glide from one character to another in the act of literary composition.

What *Nada* presents is not so much a story as a plotless series of memories, which have one overriding message: desire poses a serious threat to family unity and stability and to traditional notions of individual identity, selfhood and psychological coherence. The message is conveyed by exposing the delights of unregulated desire (sadomasochism, incest, homosexuality, violence, suicide etc.) within the context of an inverted childhood paradise, i.e. Aribau. The latter represents the 'fallen' house, the space in which — in the absence of parental authority — wild, natural, demonic forces have been unleashed and allowed to run riot, with appalling consequences. *Nada* is, in part, the account of this fascinating yet fearful return to the pleasures of pre-Oedipal sexuality, to the 'polymorphous perversity' of childhood.[12] In this regard, what is significant in the novel is that adult relations repeat the cruel play of neglected children. For example, just as Román imagines that he has Ena under his spell, she begins to jump up and down on his 'cama turca', 'Y empezaba a hacerlo [...] como cuando juego con mis hermanos' (266). Adult behaviour seems to be a perpetuation of regressive childhood intensities, signalling a desire to inhabit an unconstrained world and a refusal to grow up. Interestingly, through an apparent reversion to childish play, Ena totally subverts Román's attempts to seduce her. The trickster is humbled by one who is his match in cruelty and perversion, one whose dark, threatening side often craves release. As Ena says of herself: 'Cuando he sido demasiado sublime, tengo ganas de arañar... De dañar un poco' (264).

---

[12] As Rycroft argues, according to classical psychoanalytical theory, 'the human infant is polymorphously perverse, i.e. his infantile wishes are not canalised in any one direction and he regards his erotogenic zones as inter-changeable' (p.122); by perverse is meant 'a form of sexual behaviour in which heterosexual intercourse is not the preferred goal' (p.116).

Laforet's novel clearly recognises a need to speak of the realm of the other, of disorder, taboo, of what lies outside the dominant value system. One should perhaps admire the fact that such a novel was written by a young woman in a misogynistic, patriarchal culture, a culture of repression and sublimation, in a context of postwar social fragmentation. *Nada* reveals a concern, indeed a fascination, for the destabilizing effects of unregulated human energies in a backward, brutal society, just out of war. It displays those energies in graphic terms, records their dehumanizing effects, but only, it seems, to better accommodate and channel them into socially acceptable forms. *Nada* thus admits heroes and heroines of desire in order to subject them to the ritual of expulsion. Desire is expelled through Román's suicide or it is displaced into religion (Angustias), marriage (Ena), children (Margarita, Gloria) and writing/art (Andrea). At every point, the destabilizing force is neutralized, defused and redirected towards the reinforcement of patriarchy and traditional values. Paradoxically, Román breaks the circle of repetition, halts the cycle of victimizing women, by taking his own life, just as Angustias took herself off to the convent. His death rids Aribau of a disease which had infected patriarchy to its roots and undermined its stability and power; his suicide neutralizes the threat he posed and purifies the family atmosphere. In one sense, Aribau is exorcized of the evil which gripped it; in another, Román is a victim of a corrupt, oppressive family and class system; he is the scapegoat, whose expulsion from Aribau has a culturally stabilizing function.

Andrea, and behind her the reader, stand in awe of a figure like Román who embodies secret excess. Yet this fascination at seeing represented in Román many of the desires and lacks the protagonist (and the reader) may feel, triggers fears of psychic fragmentation and those self-preserving energies which are aimed at maintaining the stability of the social order. As dark hero of desire, Román is both an invitation and a warning; he symbolizes excess and that excess is punished. The message is that desire, the desire to experiment with those other selves, disintegrates the self, the family and society. The main task therefore is to castrate desire and deny its attractions, to channel one's energies into mature, adult, socially harmonious activities such as marriage, heterosexual relations and the family. *Nada* thus counsels restraint, control, repression; it recognizes the need to transcend childish fantasies, to make a definitive break from infantile sexuality, mother figures and their substitutes and to enter the adult world. Moreover, the sacrificial expulsion of Román makes possible a reaffirmation of social and class differences, a feature I wish to briefly develop below.

One of Laforet's main concerns in the novel is to prevent Ena from making the same mistake as her mother, i.e. to prevent her from falling in love with Román. (It is worth noting that mother and daughter are in many ways alike: for example, the thrill of sadistic behaviour, which Margarita learnt from Román, has been passed on to Ena; Román thus occurs in a modified version in Ena, reinforcing the circle of repetition. Laforet strives to break that circle and to prevent Ena repeating her mother's experience.) *Nada* thus contains a double-edged process of revenge, carried out by Ena and Gloria on Román, to exorcize in their hearts the attraction of this charismatic hero and more generally to purge the female of her desire for the dark, demonic male. In the process, what is also at stake is the need to exorcize the threat of a social inferior breaching the boundaries of a higher social class. In the various affairs Román has with Margarita, Gloria and Ena and in Andrea's fulminating reaction to the idea of marriage between Román and Ena (160), we see expressed a fear of contamination by a class inferior and an attempt to secure class boundaries. The threat of the outsider or intruder becomes a repeated structure in the novel. It occurs in the relationship between Margarita and Román (who is regarded as a dangerous 'cazador de dotes'). It also happens between Angustias and Sanz (rejected because he is the son of a mere shopkeeper), Juan and Gloria (rejected as a 'mujer nada conveniente' (27), a tainted woman of proletarian stock), Ena and Jaime (an orphan with a fortune (190), a 'niño mimado', but seen as unsuitable for a commercial family and whose identity Ena deliberately hides from her parents in order to maintain her façade as a tomboy), and between Andrea's mother and father (the unnamed father, whose family 'siempre ha sido muy rara' (25), according to Angustias, and whom Andrea's mother marries precipitously in order to escape Aribau). In other words, class interests have a powerful effect in regulating social and sexual behaviour. And even in Andrea's case, especially at Pons's party, much is made of her dowdy appearance, broken shoes and down-at-heel middle-class ordinariness. In other words, she is not equal to Pons, not fit for a boy of his station. In the end, Andrea knows her place, a feature alarmingly reinforced when she happily agrees to make coffee and sandwiches for the 'bohemios' (155-56). *Nada* explores these class divisions, especially by working through Andrea's jealousy of and admiration for Ena's supremely confident social and sexual positioning. Andrea basks in the glow of her friend's ease with young men; she is also in awe of Ena's background, which allows her a precocious, passionate and equal sexuality with men, including Román; given her own model of femininity — subservient, dutiful — this type of relationship is denied to Andrea.

Ena's class difference makes her seem much more mature and sophisticated, socially and sexually. In the course of the novel, as we have seen, Andrea idealizes Ena as the expression of all the other possible versions of female sexuality which her own petit-bourgeois niceness excludes. Given her aggressive confidence with men, Ena disrupts Andrea's romantic model and leads her to search for a form of sexual relations which will avoid normal heterosexual relations with men. And in order for Andrea to find a secure and safe sexual identity, Ena's difference has to be overcome. From being her imaginary ideal, Ena has to revert to conventional marriage with Jaime, i.e. she has to return to the social place allotted to her. No longer the femme fatale, the tomboy, the Sadeian woman, the precocious youngster attractive to older men, Ena will rediscover, through Andrea's own niceness, a side of her character she has carefully suppressed. In other words, she will go back to being the naive, submissive, feminine girl, just like Andrea. Ena's concupiscence and sensual appetite are only a front anyway, a disguise, a role she enjoys playing. So, between the two girls there is something of a sharing of personality, an exchange. While Andrea discovers Ena's

repeated encounters with Román and tries to prevent her friend from
getting hurt, Ena takes from Andrea the illusion of romance.

As mentioned at the beginning of this study, *Nada* is a novel
which begins on a note of severe disruption. Things, people,
relationships, families and identities are out of place. One of Laforet's aims in the novel is to put them back in their place. The novel
charts a passage from disruption back to harmony, a voyage during
which Andrea and the reader begin to understand the significance of
Román and Ena as representations of desiring selves, as seductive,
tabooed expressions of sexuality and femininity. The expulsion of
the one through suicide and the reversion of the other to being a nice
girl effectively neutralize the threat of those desiring alternative
selves and reaffirm the status quo. In short, Laforet writes out desire
by writing of it and in the true spirit of romance has her heroine
rescued from the maw of Aribau by her best friend and integrated
into a happy family.

Andrea's wish, of course, has always been to recover that
stable family environment of the pre-war years, which she experienced when she was seven. She longs to return to a class to which
she spiritually belongs, to a rooted, cultivated, genteel bourgeoisie.
(With regard to Aribau, Andrea is linked to her step-family through
her mother Amalia, a name that is mentioned only once in the whole
of the novel (84), in connection with a youthful photograph, which
Andrea recognizes but not her grandmother. Angustias assures
Andrea that she is part of the household and belongs: 'Pero ahora
tienes una familia, un hogar y un nombre' (58) — a name, however,
which is never divulged. Of course, given the degenerate nature of
the family at Aribau, Andrea feels little sense of loyalty or attachment.) Andrea's main problem and the stigma she has had to live
with, is that she is an orphan. She is obsessed by a lack of origins
and harbours a deep sense of inferiority and rejection. She
sublimates these lacks, especially her desire to recover her class
position, through her immersion in the literature of happy endings,
characteristic of romance. However, far from being a liberation, she
finds her move to Aribau to be yet another incarceration. She experiences the family, not as healthy and protective, but as stifling. She

finds her imagination shackled by Angustias's oppressive gaze, yet paradoxically the repression also serves to stimulate her fantasies. At Aribau, embodied in Román, she finds the cultural superiority of the decadent bourgeoisie. The problem is that it also brings with it the threat of male sexuality, with which she cannot cope. By contrast, despite their cultural poses and pretensions, which she recognizes as such, she finds the young 'bohemios' rather more acceptable, since they do not represent any sexual threat, nor do they demand that she act as a sexual being. Andrea thus finds happiness and security not within the family to which she has blood ties, but in the adopted, substitute family. To fulfil her ambition, therefore, of social mobility, she is quite happy to break family ties and reject kinship in favour of friendship; as she remarks, 'a veces pienso que es mejor la amistad que la familia. Puede uno, en ocasiones, unirse más a un extraño a su sangre' (88).

Andrea's move to Madrid is Laforet's way of reaffirming the importance of family values and unity. However important blood ties may be, Laforet seems to suggest, if they are oppressive and unfulfilling, they should be rejected. Aribau is clearly beyond the pale and is abandoned for its assumed polar opposite. The threat posed by Román, the disease of unregulated desire, is exorcized and his restless spirit is left to wander. Andrea's desired return to origins is clearly best served through her integration into a healthy substitute family, represented by Ena's household. The novel comes full circle, returning to the point of departure. Andrea repeats the cycle of confinement and release and escapes into wholeness, a leap which is derived from and projected back into literature. Not only is Andrea's departure for Madrid a happy ending. The news that Jaime and Ena are to be married simply reinforces the cloyingly romantic note of the novel's conclusion. The dramatization of desire, the struggles between negative and positive selves, the threat of metamorphosis, of psychic fragmentation, are all resolved in favour of a cosy romance ending. *Nada* thus exemplifies the triumph of literature over life, of fantasy over reality, of genre over the destabilizing effects of desire. By writing *Nada*, Laforet re-enters that fascinating 'campo de experimentación' (265), as Ena calls Aribau, and through literary types and devices re-experiences the intensities of libidinal energy, which the reader is also invited to share. But it is also through literature that desire, the enemy within, is expelled and a renovated bourgeois family and class structure reaffirmed. There remains one slightly discordant note: Andrea does not find a man. Why not? The answer seems to be that she is not in a position, as yet, to take that step. She genuinely desired romance with Pons, but showed fear of making a commitment and of having to give up the fantasies of childhood romance. As narrator, Andrea has to write out her other desiring self, i.e. the aggressive, assertive, self-confident side represented by Ena and repeated in Román. She has to engage in a kind of suicide herself, a self-murder, a violent denial of those other versions of sexuality, represented by Román and Ena, which so attracted her and made life so thrilling. As yet, she is unable to contemplate conventional marriage, even though she is physically prepared for procreation. She thus breaks the marriage cycle and settles for female friendship, or so it seems. For what is slightly disconcerting is the fact that she does not reveal whether this option is a success, whether she is still friendly with Ena and basking in the reflected love of these 'novios'. None the less, we can be fairly certain that Andrea will follow habit and return to the safety of the spectator. This is the contingent, uncommitted position from which she began the whole process of novel writing and a position she seems destined to reoccupy. Andrea is thus unable to break into adulthood and this is arguably because she is still a victim of literary fantasies, still a casualty of the genre of romance. For Andrea, making up stories is a compulsion, a drug on which she is hooked and unable to give up. One wonders, therefore, whether it is only in literature and art that she can find happiness, only in artistic creativity that she can heal the wound of childhood separation from her mother and family and enter an imaginary world of stability and androgynous wholeness.

7. Conclusion

It is difficult to reach any firm conclusions about *Nada* since, as I have found in the preparation of this study, the novel is highly derivative of other sorts of writing, but at the same time extraordinarily rich and open in its interpretative possibilities. Certainly, its fertile mixture of generic borrowings from romance, Gothic fiction, folk and fairy tales, mystery stories, confessional literature, not to mention its reminiscences of Proust, Dostoevsky and the Brontës, provide the student and critic with a wide range of positions and frameworks from which to approach the novel. Also, the fact that the account of Andrea's year at Aribau is really only part of the story and that the narrator prefers to leave unexplained what happened after her departure for Madrid is a fascinating and troubling gap in the record. It is an absence which could constitute *Nada*'s own dark double, the unwritten novel which, like a ghost, inhabits the interstices of the text presented to the reader. Besides, the reader is bound to ask whether the novel's happy ending is more apparent than real and whether Andrea has managed to break free from the circle of repetition in which she has so far been trapped. Her refusal to reveal whether life is any better in Madrid is perhaps ominous. As she points out, in her case happiness is usually short-lived: 'Pensé que cualquier alegría de mi vida tenía que compensarla algo desagradable. Que quizá esto era una ley fatal' (75).

In strict terms, *Nada* does not in fact recount the achievement of a happy ending — the story of that completion is elided. What is shown to the reader is the restoration of the conditions which will make the happy ending possible, including the purging of those unruly energies (expressed through Román and Ena mainly) which have created family and social havoc. *Nada* is thus an inconclusive, enigmatic and paradoxical novel, a confession which withholds more than it tells, a romance whose happy ending is uncertain, an exposé of deviant sexual desires in which the women are all quite innocent and redeemed and the romantic lead is incapable of fulfilling the requirements of the role.

Nada is characterized by a structural movement of repetitions and returns, a rolling programme of déjà vus, in which features from the story of one character are recycled in the story of another, in which appearances are mistaken for reality and where identities glide, merge and repeat one another in a continuous spiral. Put another way, Laforet's novel is a hall of mirrors where the self and its reflected others never quite coincide. So, is the novel fundamentally concerned with personal development and the acquisition of an identity? A reply would have to be in the affirmative, although with significant qualifications. It might be more accurate and relevant to say that *Nada* uncovers the difficulty, if not the impossibility, of achieving maturity and a stable identity. Let us not lose sight of the fact that the personal development and identity in question are those of a young woman who aspires to secure bourgeois status. As the novel shows, to become a good bourgeois woman is a potentially hazardous process and one which may never be completed.

Nada begins with the apparent fulfilment of a dream, a dream of a return to a childhood paradise; the novel thus anticipates its own narrative strategies. However, that return — to Aribau — is transformed into a nightmare. Somehow, the world has been turned upside down, rampant disorder has broken out in the garden of Eden, wholeness has been replaced by fragmentation. Aribau is filled with an air of sour hatred, manifested in aimless violence. Family relations are in turmoil. The house lacks a firm structuring principle, as if it had been abandoned by God, and the Devil were now in command. For the newcomer, Andrea, such chaos is deeply confusing yet absolutely fascinating. The main thrust of the novel will be to effect another return, i.e. to restore order, reconstruct the family, rehabilitate Ena and remove the threat of disruption posed by the misunderstood villain of the piece, Román. *Nada* thus gestures towards the aim of all romance fiction: to secure a harmonious resolution of tensions, contradictions and disorder and to return to an imaginary realm where conflicts of class and gender differences are overcome by the construction of a full, stable, female subject. However, as *Nada* comes full circle, it inadvertently exposes as a fallacy the myth which lies at the heart of bourgeois ideology, its ultimate romantic fiction: the idea of the coherent, secure self.

At Aribau, Andrea wanders through this fallen childhood paradise confronted by different role models for masculine and feminine identity. In Angustias, she finds a repressive, authoritarian figure who simply reinforces her insecurity and sense of inferiority, propelling her ever more rapidly towards the apparently liberated, seductive charms of Román. Besides, if Angustias is heaven's servant on earth, then heaven is a fearful, hierarchical, oppressive and extraordinarily dull place. By contrast, hell, championed by Román, is dazzlingly attractive and thrilling; despite his inflated, sadistic, childish ego, at least Román makes Andrea feel alive. In Ena, Andrea finds a combination of stunningly attractive, feminine good looks, a peculiar air of sexual purity, remarkable self-confidence and a malevolent, threatening streak.

Confronted by these seductive others, these powerful symbols of difference, Andrea gradually recedes as a character, fading into virtual nothingness. And given her peculiar brand of self-deprecation and masochism, she simply reinforces her lack of self-esteem by inflating and divinizing her alter egos. Ena, for example, embodies all that Andrea lacks, but Ena is also a construct, a creation of Andrea's fantasy, a projection of her desires which both produces and ratifies her own sense of inadequacy. Ena is an expression of Andrea's longing for a secure position in the family and with the opposite sex. *Nada* is full of such projections, images which only too clearly announce Andrea's lack of a secure identity. Indeed, Andrea is involved in a constant process of identity-slippage, so to speak, until there is no firm location left for her to occupy. In short, she lives in and through others; she is where she is not. Her self is thus everywhere and nowhere, in fragments, temporarily attached to this or that other identity. Moreover, the reader is invited to participate in this process of pleasurable psychic disintegration, to experience the giddy delights of trying out other possible sexual identities.

In *Nada*, therefore, the construction of a female identity is subject to a process of wishful projection and experimentation with other possible selves, embodied in other characters. The latter may appear to represent danger and aberrant sexuality, but in the end, no one is terribly naughty. The vague hints at sexual deviancy never undermine the standing of the female characters as anything other than pure and without sin. Except perhaps in the case of Ena, who is asked by Andrea whether Román made love to her: '¿Hacerme el amor? No sé' (265), replies the teenage temptress. Such a response from one who has a reputation for being hard and manipulative with her men is puzzling indeed. On a literal level, she should obviously know what happened between her and Román. Her reluctance to give a straight answer may indicate her naivety concerning the mechanics of sex and thus her true innocence in these matters. By contrast, her reply could suggest that, even though there was no physical contact, this is what she would have wished to happen. If we take into account the fact that Román is the figure whom Margarita would have preferred to marry and Ena would have had as a father, then Ena's enigmatic reply may just contain a hint of fantasies of incest, a theme which perhaps deserves further exploration. What is clear is that, sex or no sex, Andrea is unwilling to judge Ena's possible incestuous promiscuity. She refuses to comment because she is still so committed to her own particular fantasy version of Ena: strong, autonomous, incapable of giving in to Román's wiles. Of course, Andrea knows only too well that in order to find any position at all for herself, Ena's otherness has to be cancelled out, her flirtation with sexual taboos brought to an end and her apparent lasciviousness transformed into blushing femininity. The cruel, seductive, adolescent vamp, who avenges her mother's suffering and precipitates Román's suicide, has to be returned to the path of righteousness. Even without knowing it, Andrea is the passive agent of Ena's reversion. Ena is impressed by Andrea's difference, by her niceness, sentimental ordinariness and her desire for friendship: 'La amistad verdadera me pareció un mito hasta que te conocí', she reveals to Andrea (262). Ena is really a nice girl at heart and Andrea helps her to discover this other side, acting as an antidote to the 'demonios que me tenían cogida' (268), the very same 'demonios' Angustias said Andrea would never control (103). Angustias was obviously mistaken, since it is not Andrea but Ena who allows her dark side to get out of control. Ena's rehabilitation follows the path of female friendship and her reintegration into bourgeois patriarchy, after Román's demise, is signalled by her intention to marry Jaime. Here then, romance swings into action. The artful seducer kills himself, removing the source of disruption and threat and opening the way for a return to normality. The tomboy rediscovers her femininity through the example of her best female friend and plans to marry the 'niño mimado', who was earlier regarded as unsuitable. Bourgeois morality is re-established and female identity is equated with marriage, the family, childbearing and with 'las mil dulzuras del renunciamiento' (240), as Margarita pointed out. Deviant identities are written out. The happy ending is almost complete.

The interesting thing, of course, is that Andrea does not find her identity, like Ena, in a return to bourgeois normality or perhaps not quite. In a sense, she confounds Angustias's injunction that there are only two routes in life for the honest woman: marriage or the convent. Andrea follows a third route, that of female friendship. She is physically prepared for the demands of motherhood, believes that this is the path she should take but, as yet, is not quite ready to do so. For the moment, she prefers to remain in the position of observer of others, of other scenes of fulfilment, whose happiness she can share but without having to assume the attendant responsibilities. Now this is precisely the position Andrea occupied at the beginning of the novel. The reader is left with the troubling impression that she is still stuck in her specular role: 'Imposible de libertarme' (224). Andrea seems to settle for the safety of the voyeur — a position from which she writes the text of the novel and for which she has to experience something analogous to the solitude of the convent cell, thus recalling and repeating Angustias's example. Is Andrea's immersion in full-scale literary creation a sign of a full, confident, secure female identity? Or is it perhaps a form of escapism, a sign that all is not well in Madrid, a further return of the repressed, of Andrea's compulsion to fantasize and continue an almost doomed search for the lost self? My hunch is that Andrea is still in pursuit of an identity that continually eludes her, still involved in a process of identity-slippage in which she actively colludes herself. Only in literary fantasies, it seems, can she really be herself, and here we are dealing with a self that tends to be found in others. In the end, Andrea may be more of an absence than a presence, more a figment of the reader's imagination than a solid identity.

Does *Nada* convey a message to the reader? The novel certainly leaves a host of questions unanswered and this is perhaps why it is such a fascinating text. If there is a message, it has several related strands. One is that young women should avoid any entanglement in romantic illusions and beware of predatory male sexuality. Another is that a woman can best fulfil herself within the framework of marriage, family and children, a structure which helps to keep the threat of sexual temptation in check. A further strand is that even though romantic literature is dangerous and its promises are false, it can provide a safe and painless form of vicarious pleasure and entertainment. One can thus enjoy the frisson of imagined sinfulness without the complications of actual involvement. In short, sin without sex. Also, while the ultimate goal of male *Bildung* is self-discovery and the assertion of being, the goal of female *Bildung*, if *Nada* is anything to go by, is that of self-denial and the sacrifice of being. A woman's dark, desiring, disruptive self has to be kept under control, transcended, channelled into socially acceptable outlets. *Nada* shows that literature functions as one of these outlets, as a sublimation of desire and a consoling fiction. Yet, at any moment, literature might prove to be an incitement to the very desires and energies it seeks, at least on the surface, to keep at bay. This is the pleasure and the paradox of *Nada*.

Bibliographical Note

A. LAFORET'S WORKS

Nada (Barcelona: Destino, 1945)
La isla y los demonios (Barcelona: Destino, 1952)
La muerta (Barcelona: Destino, 1952)
La llamada (Barcelona: Destino, 1954)
La mujer nueva (Barcelona: Destino, 1955)
Mis páginas mejores (Madrid: Gredos, 1956)
Novelas 1 (Barcelona: Planeta, 1957)
La insolación (Barcelona: Planeta, 1963)
Paralelo 35 (Barcelona: Planeta, 1967)
La niña y otros relatos (Madrid: Editorial Magisterio Español, 1970)

B. EDITION

1. Edward R. Mulvihill and Roberto G. Sánchez *Nada*, (New York: Oxford University Press, 1958). An abridged edition, with notes and vocabulary for American college students.

C. BIBLIOGRAPHY

2. *Women Writers of Spain. An Annotated Bio-Bibliographical Guide*, ed. Carolyn L. Galerstein and Kathleen McNerney (Westport, CT: Greenwood Press, 1986). See pp.166-69 on Laforet.

D. CRITICISM

BOOKS

3. Agustí, Ignacio, *Ganas de hablar* (Barcelona: Planeta, 1974). A book of reminiscences by one of Spain's major writers which includes interesting detail concerning the award of the first Nadal Prize.
4. Cerezales Laforet, Agustín, *Carmen Laforet*. España, escribir hoy, 10 (Madrid: Ministerio de Cultura, 1982). Useful source of biographical information from Laforet's son.
5. Illanes Adaro, Graciela, *La novelística de Carmen Laforet* (Madrid: Gredos, 1971). A useful introduction to Laforet's work.
6. Johnson, Roberta, *Carmen Laforet*, Twayne's World Authors Series 601 (Boston: Twayne, 1981). Recommended as a short and sympathetic introduction.

ARTICLES

7. Chambers, Keith, "*Nada*: Nothing or Something?", *Vida Hispánica*, Vol. XXXIII, no.2 (Spring, 1984), 25-28. A short piece vindicating the literary value of Laforet's novel.
8. Collins, Marsha S., "Carmen Laforet's *Nada*: Fictional form and the Search for Identity", *Symposium*, 38 (Winter, 1984-85), 293-310. Supports the view that Andrea develops a mature and coherent identity.
9. DeCoster, Cyrus C., "Carmen Laforet: A Tentative Evaluation", *Hispania*, 40 (1957), 187-91. A short survey of Laforet's works of the 1940s and 50s, arguing that *Nada* is by far the best.
10. El Saffar, Ruth, "Structural and Thematic Tactics of Suppression in Carmen Laforet's *Nada*", *Symposium*, 28 (1974), 119-29. One of the best articles on the novel, arguing that the 'happy ending' is belied by the themes of the novel and the continuing split between narrator and protagonist.
11. Eoff, Sherman, "*Nada* by Carmen Laforet: A Venture in Mechanistic Dynamics", *Hispania*, 35 (1952), 207-11. Reads the novel in terms of a mechanistic universe in which people and objects interact haphazardly, fail to communicate and are controlled by external forces.
12. Feal Deibe, Carlos, "*Nada* de Carmen Laforet: la iniciación de una adolescente" in *The Analysis of Hispanic Texts: Current Trends in Methodology*, ed. Mary Ann Beck, First York College Colloquium (New York: Bilingual Press, 1976), pp.221-41. A psychoanalytical account, dealing with problems of sexuality and gender, arguing that despite her fears and anxieties, Andrea develops a mature personality.

13. Foster, David William, "*Nada* de Carmen Laforet (ejemplo de neo-romance en la novela contemporánea)", *Revista Hispánica Moderna*, 32 (1966), 43-55. Discusses the novel in relation to the generic features of romance literature and the Gothic novel.

14. Galerstein, Carolyn L., "Carmen Laforet and the Spanish Spinster", *Revista de Estudios Hispánicos* (Alabama), 11 (1977), 303-15. Considers the spinster figure in Laforet's work, mainly in *Nada* and in the story 'Un noviazgo'.

15. Glenn, Kathleen M., "Animal imagery in *Nada*", *Revista de Estudios Hispánicos* (Alabama), 11 (1977), 381-94. Useful overview of animal imagery, especially in relation to character portrayal.

16. Horrent, Jules, "L'Oeuvre romanesque de Carmen Laforet", *Revue des Langues Vivantes*, 35 (1959), 179-87. A broadly sympathetic survey in French of Laforet's novels (excluding *La insolación*) and her short fiction.

17. Hoyos, Antonio de, "Sobre la novela actual: Carmen Laforet", in *Ocho v.l. escritores actuales* (Murcia: Aula de Cultura, 1954), pp.25-56. Pioneering thematic survey of Laforet's long and short fiction.

18. Jones, Margaret E.W., "Dialectical Movement as Feminist Technique in the Works of Carmen Laforet", in *Studies in Honor of Gerald E. Wade*, ed. Sylvia Bowman (Madrid: José Porrúa Turanzas, 1979), pp.109-20. From a feminist perspective, argues that the repetition of character pairings across Laforet's fiction and the struggle of the female characters against repression create dialectical movement.

19. Lamar Morris, Celita, "Carmen Laforet's *Nada* as an Expression of a Woman's Self-determination", *Letras Femininas*, 1 (1975), 40-47. After briefly outlining the position and role of women in the early 1940s in Spain, argues that Andrea asserts her independence and freedom.

20. Mar, Florentina del, "*Nada* o la novela atómica", *Cuadernos de Literatura Contemporánea*, 18 (1946), 661-63. A very early piece, which criticises *Nada* for its pessimism and unchristian indifference to suffering.

21. Newberry, Wilma, "The Solstitial Holidays in Carmen Laforet's *Nada*: Christmas and Midsummer", *Romance Notes*, 17 (1976-77), 76-81. Shows the importance of two main holidays to the development of Andrea's search for romance, especially the reversal of the Cinderella story at Pons's party, and to events taking place at Aribau.

22. Ordóñez, Elizabeth, "*Nada*: Initiation into Bourgeois Patriarchy", in *The Analysis of Hispanic Texts: Current Trends in Methodology*, eds., Lisa E. Davis and Isabel C. Tarán, Second York College Colloquium (New York: Bilingual Press, 1976), pp.61-78. Traces Andrea's passage from a negative to a positive, modernised form of bourgeois patriarchy.

23. Palomo, María del Pilar, "Carmen Laforet y su mundo novelesco",
    Monteagudo, 22 (1958), 7-13. General, brief survey of Laforet's work
    up to the publication of *Novelas I* (1957).

24. Schyfter, Sara, "The Male Mystique in Carmen Laforet's *Nada*", in
    Novelistas femeninas de la postguerra, ed. Janet W. Pérez (Madrid:
    José Porrúa Turanzas, 1983), pp.85-93. Sees the development of female
    independence linked to the rejection of the romantic male.

25. Spires, Robert C., "La Experiencia Afirmadora de *Nada*", in *La novela
    española de posguerra* (Madrid: Cupsa, 1978), pp.51-73. Considers the
    relationship between the narrator and actor (the contemplative and the
    active selves) and argues for an optimistic ending, where both of these
    figures fuse into one harmonious, fully-developed character.

26. ———, "*Nada* y la paradoja de los signos negativos", *Siglo XX/20th
    Century*, Vol. 3, nos 1-2 (1985-86), 31-33. Short analysis of the
    different meanings of the term 'nada', especially in relation to Andrea's
    experience of Barcelona and the reader's experience of the novel as an
    aesthetic object.

27. Thomas, Michael, "Symbolic Portals in Laforet's *Nada*", *Anales de la
    Novela de Posguerra*, 3 (1978), 57-74. Singles out four crucial points
    or thresholds in the story, marked by symbolic entrances and exits,
    which reveal a gradual development in the protagonist towards maturity
    and independence.

28. Thompson, Currie K., "Perception and Art: Water Imagery in *Nada*",
    Kentucky Romance Quarterly, 32 no.3, (1985), 291-300. Very
    perceptive detailed analysis of water imagery and of Andrea's personal
    development as a 'prolonged baptismal experience', from which she
    emerges cured of her romantic illusions.

29. Ullman, Pierre L., "The Moral Structure of Carmen Laforet's Novels",
    in *The Vision Obscured:Perceptions of Some Twentieth Century
    Catholic Novelists*, ed. Melvin J. Friedman (New York: Fordham
    University Press, 1970), pp.201-19. *Nada* is seen as a Catholic novel
    concerning a loss of spiritual values and the moral disintegration of the
    characters.

30. Villegas, Juan, "*Nada* de Carmen Laforet o la infantilización de la
    aventura legendaria", in his *La estructura mítica del héroe en la novela
    del siglo XX* (Barcelona: Planeta, 1973), pp.177-201. Sees the novel in
    terms of 'rites of initiation' and shows how the development of the
    protagonist follows the pattern of the mythic hero of folk tales and
    quest stories, through a series of adventures towards maturity.

31. Yates, Alan, "The First-Person Narrative Mode in *La familia de
    Pascual Duarte* and *Nada*", *Vida Hispánica*, Vol. XXIV, no.3 (Autumn
    1976), 11-20. Criticises Laforet for her poor exploitation of the first-
    person narrative perspective and argues that Cela's novel shows a far
    more sophisticated use of the technique.

CRITICAL GUIDES TO SPANISH TEXTS

Edited by
J.E. Varey, A.D. Deyermond and C. Davies

CRITICAL GUIDES TO SPANISH TEXTS

Edited by
J.E. Varey, A.D. Deyermond and C. Davies